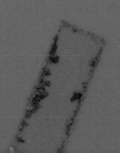

NKRUMAH

NKRUMAH

A Biography

BY ROBIN McKOWN

Doubleday & Company, Inc.

Garden City, New York

1973

ISBN: 0-385-07151-5 Trade
0-385-02778-8 Prebound
Library of Congress Catalog Card Number 77–180091
Copyright © 1973 by Robin McKown
All Rights Reserved
Printed in the United States of America

PREFACE

Ghana, the former British colony of the Gold Coast, borders the Gulf of Guinea on the West African coast. It covers an area of 92,099 square miles, about 3,500 square miles more than England, Scotland, and Wales combined. In the south is the flat coastal region. The central area is a belt of tropical rain forest, broken by streams, rivers, and densely forested hills. To the north are grasslands and savannah. The Volta is the principal river. Ghana is rich in gold, rough diamonds, bauxite, and manganese, and is the world's largest producer of cocoa.

Kwame Nkrumah led Ghana to independence under the British Commonwealth in 1957 and was its first Prime Minister. In 1960, Ghana became a republic with Nkrumah as President. His interests extended far beyond Ghana's borders. He dreamed of an Africa that was not only free but united, and was responsible for the formation of the Organization of African Unity. Although accusations of tyranny and despotism have been made against him, he remains a towering figure in African history.

CONTENTS

1   THE GOLD COAST BEFORE NKRUMAH   1
2   BOY, SCHOLAR, TEACHER   13
3   AMERICAN COLLEGE STUDENT   25
4   POLITICAL EDUCATION IN ENGLAND   34
5   GOLD COAST ORGANIZER   45
6   POSITIVE ACTION   56
7   PRISON TO PRIME MINISTER   66
8   TACTICAL ACTION   79
9   A COMMONWEALTH NATION   91
10   PRESIDENT OF THE REPUBLIC   104
11   CHAMPION OF AFRICAN UNITY   121
12   THE MILITARY COUP   134
13   EXILE   146
14   GHANA WITHOUT NKRUMAH   153
15   NKRUMAH UNFORGOTTEN   163
    BIBLIOGRAPHY   169
    INDEX   173

NKRUMAH

THE GOLD COAST
BEFORE NKRUMAH

I call Gold, Gold is mute.
I call Cloth, Cloth is mute.
It is Mankind that matters.

—Akan saying

"Gold Coast" was the name that early European traders gave to a strip of West African coastline, for the reason that the coastal Africans sold them gold. At first the name applied only to a stretch of coast about 200 miles long and extending a few miles inland.

West Africans had been mining gold since ancient times. Over the centuries a regular trade evolved between them and light-skinned Berbers of North Africa. Some West African gold is thought to have reached the North African coast when it was occupied by the Romans in the early Christian era. With the introduction of the use of the camel in about the fourth century, the trade became less hazardous. North African camel caravans crossed the Sahara Desert regularly by well-established trade routes, bringing salt and cotton cloth. In the Sudan, south of the Sahara, they were met by West African merchants with their cargoes of gold, ivory, and leather.

Several great African kingdoms grew up around the Sudan trading centers. Of these the first and most famous was Ghana. Much of what is known of the Kingdom of Ghana comes from early Arabian travelers. Their stories were remarkable. The king of Ghana received visitors sitting in his

pavilion beneath an umbrella as large as a canopy. Ten
pages, each carrying a shield and a gold-mounted sword,
surrounded him. Dogs with collars of gold and silver
guarded the king's chamber. He had a thousand horses,
each with its own carpet to sleep on, a silken rope for a hal-
ter, and three attendants to groom it. Two hundred thousand warriors, armed with iron-pointed spears or bows and
arrows, made up the Ghana army. The people of Ghana wore
gold jewelry and garments of silk and velvet or fine cotton.

Under Moslem influence, universities, libraries, and
mosques were built. Ghana became a haven of scholars and
poets and a sanctuary of learning. The kingdom's prosperity, based on taxes from the north and the south, lasted until
the eleventh century.

Ancient Ghana is important to this story, not only because
the Gold Coast Africans assumed its name when they became independent, but because it is a symbol to the African
people of their ability to build a high civilization without
European aid or guidance.

Some of the western Sudan people began to migrate
southward in the twelfth century. A number of them settled
in the central and coastal area of modern Ghana. They were
the ancestors of the Akan, the largest linguistic group in the
country. Various Akan groups spoke different dialects, but
their religion and customs were similar.

Each Akan village was governed by a council of elders,
who had the power to choose a headman or chief. At village
meetings the chief presided. He listened as each elder spoke
about the matter under discussion. When all had had their
say, the chief gave a decision, not his own but what he
judged to be the will of the people, on the basis of what the
elders had said. Even the dissenters abided by the chief's
decision.

This system prevailed in Akan society from village headmen up to paramount chiefs, the supreme rulers. By and large it was a more democratic system than that of any contemporary European nation.

Every chief, whether he ruled a small village or a kingdom, had a stool, made of precious wood and sometimes decorated with gold or silver. This was his throne, and only he could sit on it. At his death, his spirit was said to pass into the stool. It was placed in the House of the Ancestors, with stools of previous rulers. If a chief violated his trust, if he tried to impose his will on others, he could be "destooled," that is, his stool would be taken away from him and he was deposed.

The Akan believed that the sky and the earth were gods and that there were minor gods living in stones and trees and rivers. Far more intimate were their ties with their dead ancestors, whose spirits they believed still hovered around them. In ritual ceremonies, they made offerings to their ancestors, appealing to them for fruitful harvests or rain or victory in battle. Although many Akan people later adopted Christianity with genuine devotion, few of them completely renounced their ancient beliefs.

The first Europeans to meet the Akan people of the Gold Coast were the Portuguese. In 1471, two Portuguese navigators, João de Santarem and Pero de Escobar, landed on the coast. They had been sent by a Lisbon merchant to find the source of the West African gold, which was still reaching North Africa by Sahara trade routes barred to Europeans.

Beyond the white sands of the beach, the land was flat and marshy, and dotted with tall palms. Here and there were fishing villages, clusters of houses of swish, or hardened mud, and sloping thatched roofs. The Portuguese noted that the village elders who came to greet them wore golden collars and golden arm and leg bands. One chief had small gold bars intertwined with his beard. When they understood that the white men had come to trade, they willingly bartered their gold for European cloth and other goods.

More Portuguese ships came to the Gold Coast in the next decade. The Portuguese treated the African rulers with the respect due their rank. They could not afford to offend the local inhabitants, or their long, expensive and dangerous voyages would have been in vain.

In 1481, the Portuguese decided to build a fortress on the Gold Coast. In great secrecy, to avoid competition from other European powers, they sent a fleet of old transports loaded with stones and timber, already cut and prepared, along with a hundred masons and five hundred soldiers. When their ships were anchored off the coast, the Portuguese commander, Don Diego d'Azambuja, sought an audience with the African ruler they knew as Caramansa and asked his permission to build a permanent dwelling.

Caramansa, a man of great dignity, was plainly puzzled at the request, as relayed by an interpreter. Why should the white men want to live so far from their own country? He guessed, wrongly, that they had been driven out, and he tried to discourage them. Here they could find none of their accustomed luxuries, he reminded them. They could never endure the hard climate. It would be preferable if they came and went with their ships, as in the past. When men see each other only occasionally, he said, it is easier to preserve peace. But the Portuguese commander was insistent, and Caramansa finally gave his reluctant consent.

Within a few days there was trouble. Portuguese masons, while quarrying stone for their fortress foundation, destroyed a rock which harbored the spirit of a river god. The indignant Africans attacked them and were appeased only with apologies and gifts.

The fortress was completed late in 1482. It was a great white castle with towers two hundred feet high and walls thirty feet thick in some places. It became known as Elmina —the mine.

Later the Portuguese built other forts along the Gold Coast, not only to guard against possible African attacks but also to discourage their European rivals. They were, however, unable to maintain a monopoly on Gold Coast gold.

The Spaniards came but did not stay. The Dutch expelled the Portuguese for good in 1642 and took over Elmina as their headquarters. Swedes built a fortress at Cape Coast in 1657 and Christiansborg Castle at the site of modern Accra in 1659 but were driven out by the Danes. The English came and went and then returned to stay. In addition to the large fortresses, the Europeans built smaller fortified trading stations. Their outposts dotted the entire length of the Gold Coast at intervals of two to ten miles.

The forts changed hands often, by purchase or capture. In 1693, a trader of the Akwamu people, a man named Asameni, took over Christiansborg Castle from the Danes. He ruled it for several months, wore the former governor's uniform, entertained visiting sea captains, and shared the trade goods with his friends. Then he sold the castle back to the Danes for sixteen hundred pounds.

The Europeans stationed along the Gold Coast had a wretched life. Few dared venture outside their forts. The Africans tolerated their presence because of their trade goods but charged them rent—called a "Note"—for the land on which their forts stood, punished those who misbehaved, and demanded compensation for any damages. The tropical heat added to the Europeans' miseries. They fell sick with malaria and yellow fever, which they attributed to the miasma rising from the swamps. Until the benefits of quinine became known, so many perished that the Gold Coast was called the "White Man's Graveyard." Yet the lure of profit kept more Europeans coming.

In the seventeenth and eighteenth centuries, slaves took

precedence over gold as the most lucrative trade. Slavery
was not unknown among West Africans before the white
men came. More often than not the slaves were debtors or
kinsmen of debtors who had pledged them as security. They
worked as household servants and were not usually mis-
treated. A slave could marry the daughter of his master and
work his way to freedom. Some rose to high positions.

The European slave trade, which lasted two hundred
years and involved the buying and selling of millions of
African men and women, made slavery big business. African merchants on the coast sold slaves to the white men in
exchange for liquor, guns, and ammunition. The African
dealers got their supply from inland states, which also
wanted guns and ammunition. Far in the interior wars were
fought solely for the purpose of taking prisoners to meet the
needs of the white men. The effect on the economy was disastrous.

The victims, mostly the young and the strong, were
marched long distances along forest trails to the coast,
where the African merchants took over and delivered them
to European fortresses. There they were kept in dungeons,
awaiting transport. Many died in filthy and overcrowded
holds of the slave ships during the long sea journeys. The
survivors were doomed to spend their lives in servitude, usually at grueling labor in the plantations of the West Indies
or Americas.

England took the lead in the slave trade in the Gold Coast
as elsewhere in West Africa. In 1662 the British Crown gave
a charter to the Royal Adventurers of England Trading to
Africa, granting them a monopoly of trade from the Straits
of Gibraltar to the Cape of Good Hope, a charter which ignored the claims of other European nations. The Royal Adventurers built Winneba, Kommenda, and other fortresses
and took over Cape Coast from the Swedes, but by 1672
had lost all but Cape Coast to the Dutch. That year the

Royal African Company replaced the Royal Adventurers. Between 1680 and 1700 they exported 140,000 slaves. The African Company of Merchants took over in 1750. They received an annual subsidy from Britain, with the understanding that they would maintain their forts under the British flag, carry on diplomatic matters, maintain armed forces, and in general safeguard British interests. This arrangement gave political powers to a purely commercial company and had advantages for everyone except the Africans, who later called the political-business combination "imperialism."

The coastal Africans the English knew best were the Fanti, a branch of Akan people comprising many small, separate states. There were two non-Akan peoples further east on the coast—the seafaring Ga, who lived around what is now Accra, and beyond them, the Ewes, whose territory extended across the Volta River into modern Togo. Sometime in the early eighteenth century, Europeans became aware of the powerful Ashanti people, also Akan, who had their stronghold at Kumasi, in the forest region more than a hundred miles inland, and who seemed to have an insatiable craving for guns and ammunition and an inexhaustible supply of slaves and gold.

Because they did not want to pay tribute to the coastal merchants for European goods, the Ashanti had embarked on a series of aggressive wars. They had conquered the Denkyira people and captured the "Note" which entitled them to the rent of Elmina, then under the Dutch. They conquered other rival Akan nations and marched into the arid regions of the Northern Territories to subdue the primitive Dagomba people.

All the conquered peoples, once they had pledged allegiance, were accepted as part of the Ashanti nation. To symbolize their unity, the Ashanti produced a Golden Stool, said to harbor the souls of the chiefs of all the countries they had annexed. No one ever sat on the Golden Stool, not even the Asantehene, the king of the Ashanti. It rested on its side, on a Stool of its own.

In 1806, the Ashanti attacked the Fanti near the British Fort William. The British governor, Colonel Torrane, allowed two thousand Fanti non-combatants to take refuge within the fortress walls, and when the Ashanti warriors came too close, opened fire. The fire was returned, and seventeen British soldiers were wounded. In the name of free trade, which the Ashanti wanted as much as did the British, a truce was declared. Colonel Torrane delivered half of the Fanti refugees to the Ashanti and sold the others to slave ships. The Asantehene noted what he had learned about the white men: that they did not care for people.

The next year, 1807, the British government, under pressure from anti-slavery movements, ruled that Englishmen must cease trading in slaves. This was a great blow to British Gold Coast merchants. They decided to stay on only to guard their investments.

In 1830, the Committee of London sent Captain George Maclean to serve as Gold Coast governor. He was honest and capable and so just in his decisions that local chieftains brought their disputes to him. However, his good qualities worked against the Africans in the end. When the British government took over administration in 1843, there was already a basis for establishing judicial control over the neighboring African communities.

By a document known as the Bond of 1844, signed by the governor and eight chiefs, this control was formalized. The chiefs who signed acknowledged the "power and jurisdiction" of "Her Majesty's forts and settlements," and agreed that "murders, robberies, and other crimes and offences" would be tried by British officials according to British law. The Bond did not, however, grant the British Crown any territorial rights but was limited to judicial matters. It remains the only legal document that gives the British any say whatever over the Gold Coast, and Africans have pointed out that the British have repeatedly violated it.

The Ashanti again attacked the English and their Fanti allies in 1863. They won a decisive victory and returned to Kumasi. The British sent a force of soldiers after them, but so many died of tropical diseases en route that the expedition was recalled. The Africans commented: "The white man brings his cannon to the bush, but the bush is stronger than the cannon."

The Dutch, England's last European competitor, withdrew from the Gold Coast in 1869. The Africans, who had long played off one European power against the other, sensed the danger in this situation. In 1871, the Fanti united under King Ghartey IV of Winneba and formed the Fanti Confederation. Their constitution listed their aims: to develop the country's mineral resources; to make good roads; to promote agricultural and industrial pursuits; to erect schoolhouses and obtain the service of efficient schoolmasters.

Although the Fanti Confederation scrupulously observed the Bond of 1844 by acknowledging the right of Africans to appeal to British courts, the British called it a "dangerous conspiracy" and "an unlawful organization," and arrested the Federation leaders. In 1874, they formally declared the coastal area to be the Gold Coast Colony. It has been pointed out that they treated the coast as a conquered country, although it had never been conquered.

Wars continued with the Ashanti, but the superior weaponry of the white men eventually gave them dominance. In 1896, the British occupied Kumasi. There was a surrender ceremony in the great square of the city. King Prempeh, the Asantehene, took off his golden waistband and slippers, knelt before the British governor and embraced his feet in a gesture of submission. "I now claim the protection of the

Queen of England," he said. The governor demanded a huge indemnity in gold, which the Asantehene was unable to pay. He was arrested, along with the Queen Mother and the principal Ashanti chiefs. They were taken to the coast in litters and transported to the Seychelles islands to live in exile.

A new British governor, Sir Frederic Hodgson, called a meeting of Ashanti chiefs in Kumasi in 1900. He told them that their king would never return and that the British were now the supreme authority. He then demanded that they turn over to him their Golden Stool, as he now had the right to sit on it. The Ashanti chiefs found Sir Frederic's insolence unbearable. War broke out again, and it was nine months later before the Ashanti were once more subdued.

In 1902, Ashanti was declared a British colony. The same year the British moved north and annexed the Northern Territories, not because they needed this poor, barren land but to keep the French from getting it.

Ashanti, the Northern Territories, and the coastal area, called simply the Colony, composed the British Gold Coast Colony at the opening of the twentieth century. Because of its mineral resources and its growing cocoa industry, it became Britain's richest African colony next to South Africa. The British called it their African jewel.

What had started as friendly trade, when the Portuguese had first landed more than four centuries before, had finally brought the African people to complete subjugation.

Western-style education was introduced to the Gold Coast by an American missionary, Reverend Thomas Thompson. He settled in Cape Coast in 1752, rented a schoolroom to teach African children, and sent three African youths to England to continue their studies. Another Cape Coast mission school was opened in 1788 with twelve pupils. By 1820 it had five schoolmasters, four assistant teachers, of whom three were Africans, and a "lady" who taught needlework to the girls. Other mission schools sprang up along the coast.

The Swiss Basel Mission, established near Accra in the 1840s, concentrated on practical education, encouraged agricultural and local industry, experimented in cocoa growing, and built a botanical garden. Basel scholars translated the Bible into the Ga and Fanti languages. The Basel Mission seems to have been the only one that thought of education in terms of what would be valuable to the Africans rather than of what European children were taught.

A number of Africans managed to go to Cambridge and Oxford, mostly to study law. This was the beginning of the African "Coastal Elite," a sort of aristocracy. Their higher education resulted all too often in an uncritical adoration of the British system and a profound contempt for their own illiterate countrymen and the African way of life.

The British colonial service employed college-educated Africans in rather high posts up to 1860. Later on the practice was stopped. When the Europeans learned to protect themselves against malaria by draining swamps and using mosquito nets, more white men were willing to work on the Gold Coast and were given the better jobs. They brought their wives, and a British social life grew up, from which Africans were excluded.

The Coastal Elite, frustrated in their attempts to prove that they were black Englishmen, took up private law practices or became merchants. Some grew very wealthy.

In 1897, a group of coastal African lawyers, merchants, and local chieftains formed the Aborigines Rights Protection Society to protest the proposed Lands Bill, which would have given the British colonial government the right to take over what they termed "unoccupied land." By African thinking, there was no unoccupied land in the Gold Coast. It all belonged to African communities. A delegation from the Aborigines Rights Protection Society went to London to present their case. They were poorly received but because of their protests the Lands Bill was dropped.

While admittedly most of the members of the Aborigines Rights Protection Society were acting from self-interest and had little concern for the welfare of the African people, they still have the claim of being the Gold Coast's first protest organization and of having won the colony's first non-violent victory over white rulers.

2

BOY, SCHOLAR, TEACHER

I walk towards the gaudy wings of time.
—George Awoonor-Williams, Ghanaian poet

Drums were beating in the village of Nkroful when Nkrumah was born. They were not for him but were part of the funeral rites for his grandmother, his father's mother. Funerals were far more of an occasion than births among his people. When someone left the world of the living for the world of the spirits, it was customary to hold a grand ceremony lasting several weeks. New babies were not considered equally important.

According to the local priest, the date of Nkrumah's birth was September 12, 1909, just eight years after the British completed their annexation of the Gold Coast. He took so long in showing any sign of life that his mother feared he was stillborn. Her female relatives gathered around and tossed him from one to another to wake him. One of them stuffed a banana in his mouth. At once he coughed and drew a deep breath. His mother took a yelling, kicking child back in her arms.

On their police records, the British colonial government later listed him as "Francis Nwia Kofie Nkrumah, alias F. N. Kwame Nkrumah." The priest gave him his English name, "Francis." His father insisted that he be called "Nwia Kofie," after a relative. He acquired the name of Kwame, the word in his language for Saturday, because he was born on that day. The villagers knew him as Kofie. After he became Prime Minister, they made up a song about him: "When Kofie was born, they thought to cast him away, but now he rules the country." This was highly inaccurate. He was his mother's first child, and she loved him far too much to cast him away.

Nkroful, about fifty miles from the coast, in the southwestern corner of Ghana, is in the land of the Nzima. The Nzima are Akan people, though they were not allied with the coastal Fanti. They had always been peaceful. Nkrumah's mother once told him that he was descended from a great chieftain named Aduku Addai, who had settled in the region several centuries before. One young man from Nzima, Anton Wilhelm Amo, had the distinction of being the first Gold Coast university graduate on record. He was granted a doctorate of philosophy from Wittenberg University in Germany in 1733.

The cities of the coast had long had European buildings, but in Nkroful people lived much as they had before the white men came. Their houses were made of hardened mud with thatched roofs. The houses had no windows, but were built around an open bamboo compound where the family ate and worked. Cooking was done over an outside charcoal fire. Using long poles, young girls pounded a mixture of plantains, yams, and cassava in a wooden mortar to make the native dish of *fufu*. The women washed their clothes in a nearby stream and spread their colorful skirts over the bushes to dry.

Like many Gold Coast women, Kwame's mother was a trader; she added to the family income by selling rice and sugar and other small items. His father was a goldsmith who traveled from village to village, where his craftsmanship was needed. As was the custom, he had several wives. Thus though Kwame remained his mother's only child, he had a number of half brothers and half sisters. Frequently relatives came to stay. They were always made welcome, fed, and given a place to sleep. Hospitality toward kinsfolk or tribal comrades is an ancient custom in most of Africa, one which colonial rule did not alter.

Most of what is known of Nkrumah's childhood comes through his own memories, related in his autobiography. One of these early memories was of a trip with his mother to the coastal town of Half Assini where his father was then working. They walked all the way, and it took them six days there and back. When there was no village near at nightfall they slept in the open, making a fire of twigs and dried leaves to keep wild animals away.

Half Assini was separated from the Ivory Coast, a French colony, by the Tano River. Nzima people lived on both sides of the river. When Nkrumah and his mother visited friends across the boundary, they skirted around the shore to avoid red tape and questioning by the custom authorities. The absurdity and inconvenience of such arbitrary boundaries struck Kwame at an early age.

He was not quite four when a British cargo ship, the *Bakana*, ran aground off the Nzima coast and buried her propeller in several feet of sand. The captain was drowned. People claimed the disaster was caused by the god of the river, Ama Azule, who wanted a ship of his own to visit the goddess of a creek, Awianaluanu. In the following months, the *Bakana* shifted her position toward Ama Azule. No one was surprised. For years the empty hull stayed on the shore, but it was common knowledge that if strange lights appeared on the sea at night, the god was piloting his ship back and forth to his goddess.

The river gods were very real to the Nzima people who had lost none of their faith in the power of their ancestors. Kwame heard many times how ancestors could bring good fortune to those who showed them respect and could punish those who neglected them. The tales did not frighten him. He dreamed of the day when he, too, would be a ghost, able to pass through walls and closed doors and sit unobserved at family meetings.

Children had a great deal of freedom in Nkroful. Kwame's mother, a quiet, dignified woman, rarely scolded him. He remembered her punishing him only once. That was when he had a tantrum and spit into their pot of stew.

He and his playmates had no factory-made toys, but once two of his older half brothers built a model of a bicycle out of two iron hoops. They let him be the first to sit on it, an occasion he never forgot. For the most part the children found their fun playing along the lagoon or in the forest. Sometimes young Kwame left the others and went off by himself in the woods, where he sat quietly, listening to the songs of birds and watching the small animals. He built traps to get pets—a land crab, a squirrel, a bird, and a rat.

Kwame was five when the First World War broke out in Europe. By this time the European powers had divided up all Africa—with the exception of Liberia and Ethiopia—as though it were a piece of pie of which each had the right to a slice. Britain had the largest share, about a third of the continent. Now England called on her African colonies to help her win the "war to make the world safe for democracy." A Gold Coast regiment served with distinction in a campaign against German Togoland and the Cameroons in West Africa and later in German East Africa.

After Germany's defeat, her African colonies were divided up among the Allies in the form of a mandate granted by the League of Nations. Part of England's spoils was a strip of Togoland of about 13,000 square miles along the western border of the Gold Coast, beyond the Volta River. (The rest of Togoland went to France.) This became a fourth province of the Gold Coast, the Trans Volta/Togo territory. The Ewe people living in the Gold Coast proper were thus united with those in the new territory but were cut off from Ewes in French Togoland.

The war affected Kwame Nkrumah very little. In the midst of it, his parents enrolled him in a Roman Catholic mission school. Illiterate themselves, they were determined that their son should have the education they had missed. Education was not free even in a mission school. Parents had to pay a fee and buy textbooks. Kwame helped by raising a few chickens to sell.

His teacher was a firm believer in not sparing the rod. The boys were whipped for the slightest disobedience. One day when a school inspector was due, they decided to get their revenge by playing truant. All day they ran wild, roaring with laughter at the thought of their teacher's expression when he had to show the inspector an empty classroom. The teacher of course had the final say. The next day each truant received forty-eight lashes.

Kwame's father had little interest in Christian religion. His mother was a Catholic, while still retaining the beliefs of her people. The director of the mission school, a wealthy Catholic priest, Father George Fisher, took a special interest in Kwame, encouraged him with his studies, and persuaded him to be baptized in the Roman Catholic Church. Kwame served the Mass and took his religious duties seriously.

After he graduated from the mission school with the rough equivalent of a grammar school education, he stayed on as a pupil-teacher. He was then seventeen but so small that he had to stand on a stool to teach. Because of the shortage of qualified instructors, pupil-teachers were not uncommon. Often the pupil-teachers themselves had not mastered much English grammar. As late as 1952, the American writer Richard Wright, visiting a schoolroom on the coast, heard a young teacher conjugating the verb "to go": "I go; you go; he no go." Nkrumah must have been far above the average, for he was found eligible for a scholarship at the Government Training College, a teachers' preparatory school in Accra.

Accra, capital of the Gold Coast Colony, was originally settled by the Ga nation, and its African population was still largely Ga-speaking. On the outskirts was Christiansborg Castle, now the residence of the British governor. Accra had no harbor. Ships anchored far out, while African longshore-men, stripped to the waist, paddled canoes back and forth with ingoing and outgoing cargo.

The city itself was a jumble of the old and the new, of tumble-down slums in the Jamestown section, new white office buildings, their paint already peeling, in the business districts, and elegant mansions in the British residential district. Along the streets were tables heaped with merchandise, presided over by market women in turbans, large earrings, bracelets, and long wraparound skirts of vivid colors and striking patterns. Men wore Western suits or flowing robes of peacock colors, or short tunics in the style of the Northern Territories. There was bustle, noise, laughter, shouting. Crowds were everywhere. For Nkrumah, the effect was terrifying.

His classmates recognized him as a poor country boy and tormented him unmercifully. In the midst of the nightmare of his first weeks, he received word that his father had died of blood poisoning. With his principal's permission he went home but arrived too late for the funeral ceremonies. His father's death broke up family life as he had known it. His mother went to stay with his father's brother, in accordance with the custom that a widow becomes the responsibility of her late husband's nearest of kin. She apparently was not happy there, for later she returned to Nkroful.

Back at school, Nkrumah stuck to his studies and finished his first year, when the Government Training College became part of Achimota College and he was transferred there.

Achimota was the Gold Coast's first institution on a secondary or high school level. It had been built by the progressive governor, Sir Gordon Guggisberg, over the objections of the Colonial Office in London, which opposed mass education for Africans on the grounds that it would destroy their "tribal" outlook. The school had an attractive campus and residential units, a museum, a swimming pool, a demonstration farm, and a model village. Most of the Achimota professors had Oxford or Cambridge degrees. Nkrumah's near-accidental admission there placed him among the most privileged of African youth.

Guggisberg, of whom Nkrumah must have heard a great deal at Achimota, had been sincerely interested in giving Africans a chance to help rule their own country. Before he arrived in 1919, the Governor's Executive Council and Legislative Council, which corresponded to the British Cabinet and House of Parliament, were all composed of men nominated or appointed by the governor, who was himself appointed by the British Crown. The Legislative Council occasionally had a few African members, carefully chosen for their sympathy to British policy, but these men had no power to do anything except to offer an opinion.

During Guggisberg's administration, the Legislative Council was enlarged to include nine non-official African members. Three of them were elected by taxpayers in Accra, Kumasi, and Cape Coast. This set the precedent of giving at least a limited vote to the African people. The other six members were chosen by the Provincial Councils of Chiefs, created by Guggisberg as a sort of electoral college.

In administering the country, the British worked through local chieftains, to whom they entrusted the collection of taxes and other small chores. Guggisberg promoted this system, known as Indirect Rule, since theoretically it allowed

Africans to retain the structure of their former nations. In practice, it turned the chieftains into puppet rulers whose first obligation was to the British rather than to their own people. The British had a great deal of trouble controlling the Akan who, with their democratic heritage, considered it their right to de-stool any chief who did not look after their best interests. Indirect Rule was also an invitation to corruption, hitherto unknown. Not all the tax money the chiefs collected reached the British coffers. And some chiefs accepted "gifts" in return for certain favors. While the Coastal Elite were already thinking of running the Gold Coast government themselves, most of the chiefs were quite content with British rule and their own favored position under it.

In 1925, Sir Gordon Guggisberg brought back King Prempeh I of the Ashanti after his quarter of a century exile in the Seychelles islands. He was reinstated not as the Asantehene, king of the Ashanti, but as the Kumasihene, chief of Kumasi, once the capital of the entire Ashanti nation. Six years later, when the old king died, he was replaced by his nephew, Prempeh II, then a storekeeper in Kumasi, and the title of Asantehene was restored to him. It was an empty honor. He had the trappings of his ancestors—the big umbrella, the attendants, and the ceremonial dress—but the glory and grandeur of the Ashanti kingdom were gone.

Most of Nkrumah's classmates at Achimota were either sons of the Coastal Elite or sons of chiefs. Nkrumah may have been aware of the rivalry between the educated aristocracy of the coast and the mostly illiterate chiefs, but it did not concern him directly. These two groups made up only a small minority of the Gold Coast population. Nkrumah belonged to the majority group—the poor, the disenfranchised, the exploited. Their very numbers would one day make them the most powerful group of all.

The vice-principal of Achimota was Dr. Kwegyir Aggrey, under whom Nkrumah took a course in African studies. Aggrey was an African scholar of great vitality and charm, with the courage to express ideas seldom voiced before in the Gold Coast. He considered it an honor to be black and felt that racial segregation was an abomination. Whites and Blacks should work together, he said. It took both Black and white keys on a piano to produce harmony; it was the same with people. Nkrumah became utterly devoted to him.

One day Dr. Aggrey joined Kwame and two other students in the empty school auditorium. He joked with them for a few minutes and then announced he was leaving on an extended trip to England and America. Suddenly he grew serious. Up until now, he said, he had only been able to make them hungry. Perhaps after he came back he would be able to satisfy their hunger. He made it clear that he was not talking about physical hunger but about hunger for freedom. Nkrumah never saw him again. Several months later, he died in America.

Nkrumah's fierce loyalty was evident in a dispute he subsequently had with the professor who took over Dr. Aggrey's course in African studies. The professor was discussing the various peoples who make up Africa—the Tuaregs in the Sahara, the Pygmies in the Congo basin, the Hottentots in the south. Nkrumah shot up his hand.

"I don't agree with you," he said and quoted Dr. Aggrey to the effect that all Africans were one people from north to south.

The professor tried to explain that there were differences among Africans in traditions as well as in physique and appearance. Nkrumah remained unconvinced. When he later learned for himself that such differences did exist, they remained inconsequential as far as he was concerned. For him, Africans were always one people.

Nkrumah studied hard at Achimota, especially educational psychology, mathematics and Latin, but he also found time for other activities. He went in for track. He joined a group of Fanti and Nzima students who gave performances of tribal dances. In his third year he took the leading role in a play called *Kofi Goes Abroad*. Based on a popular theme in colonial Africa, it was about a young African doctor who returned after his studies abroad and won over the suspicious villagers by curing a man with a fever whom the local witch doctor had been unable to help.

Nkrumah's favorite activity was debating with fellow members of the Aggrey Students' Society, formed in honor of Dr. Aggrey. He relished taking the minority side of a debate and then trying to win over his audience to an unpopular point of view. In the classroom he used the same skills when arguing with his professors. At least one of them was sufficiently annoyed to dismiss him as "an impossible chap." Others icily reminded him that he was, after all, at Achimota to learn and not to teach.

In 1930 at the age of twenty-one, he graduated from Achimota and promptly accepted a teaching post at the Roman Catholic Junior School at Elmina, the town named after the first Portuguese fortress. He enjoyed working with the children and helped to form a teachers' association, aimed at improving conditions for underpaid schoolteachers.

One of the speakers who addressed the association was the Nigerian, Nnamdi Azikiwe, who had been educated in the United States and who was now living in Accra and writing eloquent articles about African nationalism in the *African Morning Post*. Azikiwe was to serve as President of the independent Republic of Nigeria from 1963 to 1966.

The next year Nkrumah was transferred to the post of head teacher at the Roman Catholic Junior School at Axim in Nzima land, a town of which the scholar and explorer Sir Richard Burton had once written: "there is nothing more picturesque upon this coast." At Axim, Nkrumah became active in the Nzima Literature Society. A photograph of the Society's members, taken at the time, shows a group of middle-aged and elderly Africans, one in the white robes of a priest, several in native dress, and the others in contemporary European dress.

One of the Society members was Dr. Samuel R. Wood, a very old man who had gone to London in 1897 as a delegate of the Aborigines Rights Protection Society to fight the Lands Bill. As one of the Coastal Elite, he had considerable contempt for the uneducated and often unscrupulous chiefs the government was favoring under the system of Indirect Rule. Nkrumah enjoyed listening to him reminisce and learned a good bit from him about Gold Coast political history.

In 1931, Nkrumah went to Accra to take his examinations to enter an English university. He failed in mathematics and Latin, the two subjects he had tried so hard to master. It was a disappointment but not an unexpected one. Had his parents been rich enough to afford to send him to an English preparatory school, he might have had a better chance. English university standards were extremely difficult to meet for Africans with only a secondary school education. Nkrumah's friend Dr. Wood proposed that he try America where entrance requirements were not so strict and where he could work and help pay his expenses, which would be impossible in England. Nkrumah needed little urging to write to the address Dr. Wood gave him—Lincoln University, Pennsylvania—and apply for admission.

He spent one more year as a teacher, at the Roman Catholic Seminary at Amissano, near Elmina, which trained novices for a religious vocation. He considered becoming a Jesuit priest, but he wanted even more to go to America. Lincoln University had sent him an application blank, which he had diligently filled out, but he had heard nothing more. Moreover, with all his efforts to be economical, he had saved only a few pounds.

One day he stowed away on a ship going to Lagos, Nigeria, where he had a prosperous uncle. Members of the crew fed him and kept him hidden. He arrived shabby and dirty, but his uncle received him kindly, as his parents had always welcomed their poor relatives. Before he left, his uncle loaned him enough for his fare to America and about thirty pounds extra.

On March 1, 1935, he again wrote to Lincoln University. Since he had written a year before, he said, he had been making arrangements to come to America. He was now prepared to sail, "if only a ray of hope will come from you." Not long afterward the university sent him an admission card.

3

AMERICAN COLLEGE STUDENT

I am learning, let me succeed.
—Prelude to Akan drummer's song

In August 1935, Nkrumah set sail from Takoradi Harbor, the Gold Coast's only deep-water port, built under the administration of the visionary Sir Gordon Guggisberg. As his ship glided past the long docks and great cranes, he caught a last glimpse of the Gold Coast of his childhood, the mud-thatched huts, the children wading and women washing their clothes and bathing in a small stream. It would be twelve years before he saw these familiar sights again.

He wandered down to his third-class cabin and sat on a bunk, annoyed that he, a full-grown man of twenty-six, should feel so lost and homesick. A telegram was waiting for him there from his Nigerian friend, Nnamdi Azikiwe. "Trust in God and in yourself," it read; the message cheered him.

The ship landed in Liverpool, a bustling, gloomy industrial city which had grown rich from the African slave trade. Between 1783 and 1793, a recorded 878 Liverpool ships had transported 303,737 West African slaves to the New World, with an estimated profit of 17 million pounds sterling. It perhaps struck Nkrumah as ironic that now, a hundred and fifty years later, he was headed for this same New World of his own free will, to seek an education unavailable in his own land.

Since there was no American consulate in the Gold Coast, he had to get his visa from the American embassy in London. He spent two weeks there waiting for his passport to be properly stamped. On October 2, the London streets were filled with newsboys shouting that Mussolini of Italy had launched a full-scale attack on Ethiopia, a country that thus far had resisted European domination.

Haile Selassie, the Ethiopian Emperor, had foreseen the invasion and had twice appealed to the League of Nations to impose sanctions on Italy and to provide help against Italian aggression. He had also tried to buy arms and ammunition in Europe. It was no use. His troops, mostly barefoot and armed with spears or ancient muskets, confronted a modern motorized army equipped with the most up-to-date weapons. His defenseless people were subjected to the first air bombings in history and to the horrors of mustard gas.

Nkrumah walked the London streets in anger. People around him, intent on their own affairs, showed no emotion. Were they blind to the evils of colonization? Or didn't they care? He felt as though England had declared war on him personally.

It was the end of October before Nkrumah reached New York. He stayed two days with a Lincoln University graduate from Sierra Leone who now lived in Harlem, then went on to the university. Classes had already started, and he feared he would be refused admission.

On his arrival he reported promptly to the dean, the Reverend George Johnson, to explain the delay caused by his troubles getting a visa. In answer to one of the dean's questions, he confessed that he had only a little over a hundred dollars and intended to work for his expenses. The dean finally agreed to let him enter as a probationer. If he did well in the forthcoming examinations he would become a full-fledged freshman.

Lincoln University, near the small town of Oxford in southeastern Pennsylvania, had been opened for "male Negroes" in 1857. It was founded by Presbyterians, and in addition to its liberal arts college had a theological seminary. The students were mostly American, but there was a sprinkling of Africans. One of them, Ako Adjei, was a Gold Coaster of the Ga people from Accra. He was a talkative, friendly young man with considerable talent as a journalist, and he became Nkrumah's close friend.

Nkrumah worked extraordinarily hard those first months and passed his examinations easily. Indeed his grades were high enough to entitle him to a scholarship, which provided him with a small sum at the beginning of each semester. It was testimony not only to his own diligence but to his Achimota training. Also in his freshman year, he won second prize and a medal in an oratorical contest.

Even with his scholarship, he had to earn more money to get by. He worked in the school library, which he enjoyed, and as a waiter in the dining hall, which was less pleasant. Later on, he wrote papers on sociology and economics for students too indolent to do their own. His standard fee for such papers was a dollar each.

On his first summer vacation, he joined his Sierra Leone friend in Harlem. In spite of President Roosevelt's expansive work projects, jobs were still scarce in America in the wake of the Great Depression. To his astonishment, Nkrumah saw people searching garbage cans for bits of food.

He and his friend decided to buy fish and poultry from the early morning markets and sell them on the street corners, but they could not manage to break even. Nkrumah developed a rash; it turned out he was allergic to handling fish. Their enterprise lasted only two weeks.

Next Nkrumah worked in a soap factory, loading rotting entrails and lumps of fat into a wheelbarrow and wheeling his repulsive cargo to the processing plant. He could not eat, lost weight, and fell sick. His West Indian landlady looked after him until his health returned. Hard times followed.

On a hunch he joined the National Maritime Union and signed up for work on summer cruises. He found a job as a dishwasher aboard the *Shawnee,* which journeyed between New York and Vera Cruz. The next summer he served table in the officers' mess. The year after that he became a bell-hop; he wore a uniform and a pillbox hat and passengers gave him tips. It did not seem important what kind of work he had to do, so long as he could stay in college.

In his second year he was invited to join the Beta Sigma Fraternity, which had as a motto, "Culture for Service and for Humanity." There was nothing of culture, service, or humanity in the initiation ceremony, during which he was chased across the field like a fox, captured, spanked, and pushed blindfolded into a thorny hedge.

Nkrumah had several attractive girl friends in America but he did not think of marrying, settling down, and having children, like other young men his age. He was preparing himself for the future. He had already concluded that it was his destiny "to return to Africa and join in the stuggle for its liberation from the tentacles of imperialism."

In 1939, he graduated as a Bachelor of Arts, with his major in philosophy. A verse appeared about him in the class yearbook:

> Africa is the beloved of Nkrumah's dreams;
> Philosopher, thinker with forceful schemes.
> In aesthetics, politics, he's in the field,
> Nkrumah, "tres interessant" [very interesting]
> radiates appeal.

In a photograph taken of Nkrumah at this time, he looks very earnest and much younger than his thirty years. His lips are full and sensitive, his eyes wistful, his forehead unusually high. He wears glasses, which he later discarded.

He still owed the university money. The authorities had been lenient and given him extra time, but the debt weighed heavily on him. There exists, in the university files, a series of letters from him to Dean Johnson written over the next several years, promising to pay the money as soon as possible, expressing his worry about it, and asking how much still was left to be paid. In these letters he signed himself either "Francis Nkrumah" or "F. Nwia-Kofi Nkrumah."

In a letter written the summer after he graduated, he listed the books he had been reading: Joad's *Guide to Philosophy;* Will Durant's *Story of Philosophy;* Kant's *Critique of Pure Reason* ("a hard nut to crack"); the works of Descartes, Schopenhauer, Nietzsche, and Spinoza, which he summed up as "complicatingly interesting." He was also "captured" by "the ethics of Ibsen and Tolstoy." More than anything else, the listing shows the extent of his intellectual curiosity.

During this period Nkrumah began reading the works of Karl Marx and Lenin to help, as he said, "resolve the problem of imperialism." He was fascinated by a little-known work called *Philosophy and Opinions of Marcus Garvey.*

Garvey, a Jamaica-born black and flamboyant figure, had come to America in 1914 and organized the Universal Negro Improvement Association, intended to promote unity between Africans in many lands and to improve conditions in black communities everywhere. He called himself "Leader of the Negro Peoples of the World" and used as his slogan "Africa for the Africans." Garvey raised a considerable amount of money for a shipping line between New York, Jamaica, and Africa, to take Africans back to Africa, a shipping line that never materialized. Nkrumah always gave Garvey credit for promoting unity among black peoples, but he later discarded Garvey's philosophy, based in principle on black racial segregation. "Africa for the Africans" does not mean that other races should be excluded from Africa, he said in one of his many speeches. "It only means that Africans shall and must govern themselves in their own countries."

At Dr. Johnson's suggestion, Nkrumah entered Lincoln Theological Seminary in the fall of 1939. That his own background was Catholic and the seminary was Presbyterian did not bother him. The different sects into which white people had divided up Christianity was not, after all, his concern. He called himself "an undenominational Christian." On Sundays he often preached in black churches, which he enjoyed immensely. "The work is hard but the thrill of accomplishment is worth the effort," he wrote.

One of his seminary assignments was to make a "socio-religious survey" of black Americans living in Pennsylvania. For his research he visited over six hundred Pennsylvania homes. He was appalled by their poverty. In his first flush of enthusiasm for America, he had accepted the country as a land of equal opportunity for all. He could no longer ignore the fact that people with dark skins had less opportunity than others.

Personally he met with great kindness from many Americans, black and white. That there were restaurants and other public places where he was not welcome, he learned the hard way. On one journey from Philadelphia to Washington, his bus stopped at Baltimore. He was thirsty and asked the waiter at a refreshment stand for a glass of water. The man scowled and said that the place for people like him was in the spittoon outside. It was the rudeness of the affront that shocked him most. The British in the Gold Coast preserved their aloofness, often with an icy reserve, but they were not impolite.

America entered the Second World War on December 7,

1941, to fight with the Allies against Hitler in Europe and against the Japanese in the Pacific. The European theater of the war had already spilled over into Africa, as had happened in the First World War. Nkrumah must have read with pleasure how Emperor Haile Selassie and his guerrillas, with aid from British troops, had set Ethiopia free. Letters from home would have told him that regiments from the Gold Coast were fighting in North Africa and in distant Burma. The war's main effect on Nkrumah was that the summer cruises on which he had sailed as dishwasher, waiter, and bellhop, were canceled for the duration.

With the encouragement of Dr. Johnson, he enrolled in the University of Pennsylvania graduate school, and three times a week traveled the fifty miles to Philadelphia to take graduate courses in philosophy and education. There he helped to found an Institute of African Languages and Culture, at a time when African studies were as neglected in America as they were in colonial Africa.

More and more he thought in terms of action and organization, of the need for black people to join together and show their strength if they were ever to get their just due. He organized a branch of the African Students' Association, started in Canada, expanded it to include non-students, and in September 1942 presided over the first General Conference of Africans in America. With his Gold Coast friend, Ako Adjei, he edited a magazine called *The African Interpreter*, to let American blacks know about the sufferings of their brothers in colonial Africa.

Early in 1943, he attended a memorial service for Dr. Kwegyir Aggrey, held in Salisbury, North Carolina, where he had died. At his tomb, his Gold Coast compatriots went through the ritual of a libation, pouring wine on the ground drop by drop, in honor of the ancestors. The dean of Lincoln University read about it in *The African Interpreter* and wrote Nkrumah a stern and reproachful letter, expressing his "utter surprise" at Nkrumah's participation in a non-Christian rite.

Nkrumah answered him on April 24, saying that no written explanation would do him justice but that when he came back to Lincoln he would talk about the matter at length. He also wrote that he wanted his life to be a symbol of what was best both in Christianity and in the laws, customs, and beliefs of his own people. He would always remain a Christian, he said, but he hoped not a blind Christian.

After having graduated from the Lincoln Theological Seminary as a Bachelor of Sacred Theology in 1942, Nkrumah lived in Philadelphia, studying full time at the University of Pennsylvania graduate school. He received a master of arts degree in philosophy, then spent another year to get his master of science degree in education.

More and more often he was invited to speak at public meetings. He talked mostly about Africa, sometimes about the wrongs of colonialism and sometimes about ancient African kingdoms. To people brought up on the notion that Africa was steeped in barbarism before the arrival of the white man, his speeches must have been a revelation. At Howard University he successfully challenged the conventional views of Africa's past propounded by a noted white anthropologist. His reputation spread, both as an African scholar and as a champion of the oppressed peoples of his race. Toward the end of his stay in America he met many prominent black citizens, among them Paul Robeson, Richard Wright, and Dr. William E. B. Du Bois, co-founder of the National Association for the Advancement of Colored People.

In the winter of 1944, Nkrumah took a night job at the Sun Shipbuilding Yard in Chester, Pennsylvania, to supplement his always uncertain income. Sometimes it was so cold that his hands stuck to the steel. At eight each morning he returned to his lodgings, ate breakfast, slept briefly, then continued the research on his doctor's thesis. He had made little progress on it before he fell ill with pneumonia and had to be taken to a hospital in an ambulance and put in an oxygen tent. During his convalescence all he could think of were the flowers, the palms, the tropical temperatures of Africa. He had been in America for nearly ten years. It struck him as long enough.

Resisting the temptation to return to the Gold Coast at once, he arranged to go to London, with the aim of completing his doctor's thesis, and perhaps studying law there as his friend Ako Adjei was doing. The more he could learn he reasoned, the more help he could give his country when he did go back.

Many years later an American missionary asked Nkrumah his most striking impression of the United States. "The energy . . ." he said immediately. "How everybody tries to better his condition."

He did not remain among Americans for ten years without acquiring some of their qualities. American slang became part of his vocabulary. For some time to come he spoke English with an American accent. In America too, he seems to have developed a certain defiance of what is now called the Establishment, a refusal to be impressed with people merely because of their rank or wealth. It was this distrust of authority that would enable Nkrumah to fight for his convictions, regardless of how highly placed his adversaries were.

4

POLITICAL EDUCATION
IN ENGLAND

Only the best is good enough for Africa.

—KWEGYIR AGGREY

For some time Nkrumah had been corresponding with George Padmore, a West Indian journalist living in London, whose writings he greatly admired. Padmore was a true revolutionary who refused to accept any political labels. He was completely dedicated to the cause of freeing nonwhite people from the ties that had bound them for centuries. Nkrumah had told Padmore the date and time his train from Liverpool would reach London's Victoria Station. To his delight the West Indian writer was there to greet him.

It was June 10, 1945, two months after the death of President Roosevelt and one month after Germany had surrendered unconditionally to the Allies. In San Francisco, representatives from many nations were meeting to draw up the charter for the United Nations. A new era had begun.

Padmore took Nkrumah straight to the headquarters of the West African Students' Union, organized to help African students abroad. They found him a room. He got in touch with Ako Adjei and other old friends. Through Padmore he quickly made new ones. It was a contrast to his first London visit when he had been alone and friendless.

His room was cold and dark, and he soon set out in search of something more cheerful. In crowded post-war London, lodgings were hard to come by. Even where there was a For Rent sign, he was turned away because of his dark skin. One landlady refused him, not for herself, she said, but because she had her "other gentlemen to consider."

A pleasant-faced woman finally rented him a small, clean room with no hesitation at all. He lived there for the rest of his stay in London. When he came home at midnight or later, as often happened, his landlady left food in the oven. In exchange he washed her dishes.

His original plan was to get his doctorate thesis in philosophy, on the subject of "logical positivism," and then to take up law. To further his first aim, he enrolled at the London School of Economics as a post-graduate student. There his research was supervised by the brilliant political science professor Harold Laski, who influenced some of the brightest young men of his time, both in England and at Harvard in America. But Nkrumah never did complete his thesis, nor did his law studies get off the ground. Within a few weeks he was deeply involved in political activity.

George Padmore enlisted him as a volunteer to prepare for the Fifth Pan-African Congress, scheduled to be held in Manchester in October. Night after night they sat up in Padmore's small kitchen with a pot of tea before them, writing letters to African organizations in Africa and the West Indies, urging them to send delegates. It was curiously exciting to correspond with so many people who had the same interests.

As far as is known, a barrister from Trinidad named H. Sylvester Williams had coined the term "Pan-African." Under his sponsorship a Pan-African Conference was held in London in 1900. William Du Bois, who had attended the conference as a young man, later became known as "the father of Pan-Africanism," and it was Du Bois who took a leading role in the series of Pan-African Congresses that followed.

The first Pan-African Congress was held in 1919 in Paris. It adopted a resolution proclaiming the need for reform in the treatment of Africans and advocating that Africans be allowed to share in the government of their countries "as fast as their development permits." Nothing was said of possible independence.

The second Congress, held in two sessions in London and Brussels in 1921, was similarly concerned with colonial reform. The third Congress, held in 1923 in two sessions in London and Lisbon, contained in its manifesto the touching sentence: "In fine, we ask in all the world, that black folk be treated as men." This Congress was attended by Dr. Harold Laski and the British writer H. G. Wells, and received a message of encouragement from Ramsay MacDonald, British Prime Minister. The fourth Congress took place in New York in 1927, the only time one was called in America.

Eighteen years had passed since then. Times had changed. Britain and France had acknowledged that the pattern of eighteenth-century colonialism was outmoded. The fifth Pan-African Congress in Manchester was larger than the preceding ones, and the texture of its membership was different. Dr. Du Bois, the gray-haired, eloquent champion of American blacks, presided once again, but the American and West Indian contingents were eclipsed by a number of still unknown young men from Africa. Besides Nkrumah there were Johnstone Kenyatta, who as Jomo Kenyatta would become Kenya's Prime Minister and President; the South African novelist Peter Abrahams; Dr. Raphael Armatto, a poet from Togoland; Wallace Johnson, a Sierra Leone trade unionist and journalist. Also present were some young Gold Coast Africans, who would later serve under Nkrumah in a free Ghana.

For the African contingent, talk of reform, of treating "black folk" as men was no longer enough. For the first time at a Pan-African Congress, there was a forthright denunciation of colonialism as "a systematic exploitation of the economic resources" of the dominated countries, ". . . by imperialist Powers to the detriment of the inhabitants." Independence was no longer a forbidden word: "We demand for Black Africa autonomy and independence . . . We are determined to be free."

The Congress resolutions spoke of "one man, one vote," a shocking idea for the old-school colonial administrations. There was no mention of communism, or of socialism, but the resolutions condemned "the rule of private wealth and industry for private profit alone." If the Western world was still determined "to rule Mankind by force," then Africans "as a last resource" might have to respond by force to achieve their freedom. The hope was expressed that this "last resource" would not prove necessary. Far preferable was a course of "Positive Action," the passive resistance practiced by Mahatma Gandhi in India.

These were intoxicating words for Nkrumah. After the Manchester Congress, he returned to London afire with enthusiasm. Along with several friends he founded the West African National Secretariat. The avowed aim of this organization, in which he served as secretary, was to bring together the nationalist leaders of all the West African colonies, so that they could share their problems and work out a program of action.

A small room on Gray's Inn Road became headquarters of the secretariat. It was unheated but had a fireplace. The members scoured the streets for lumps of coal which had fallen from coal trucks or spilled over when the trucks filled coal bins. Some English girls volunteered to type letters. The secretariat's headquarters became a gathering place not only for Africans but for anybody sympathetic to their cause.

Sometimes the members adjourned to a small working-class cafe on Tottenham Court Road, where they continued their endless discussions over a pot of tea and a roll. To the credit of the proprietor, he let them stay as long as they wanted no matter how little they ordered.

Part of the secretariat's work was to inform the British public of the truth about the exploitation of Africans by white rulers. To this end, Nkrumah wrote newspaper articles and pamphlets and spoke at open meetings. The English people had been told so long and so often about the noble work of missionaries in Africa that they had the impression the British were there simply to bring Christianity and "civilization" to the heathen. They had trouble believing that the main results of white occupation were poverty and humiliation for the Africans.

Some Labour Members of Parliament gave the secretariat their full support. A sympathizer arranged a party to introduce other Labour officials to the leading West Africans, Nkrumah among them. Nkrumah had a long talk with one Labour parliamentarian, the Honourable Geoffrey Bing, who was very knowledgeable about Gold Coast history. Nkrumah was impressed with the fact that Bing showed no trace of feelings of racial superiority. Before he left the party, Nkrumah promised to send Bing one of his pamphlets. In the press of other matters it slipped his mind, but he did not forget their conversation.

Nkrumah published three major pamphlets in London. Two of them had to do with the need for higher standards of education in the colonies. The third, *Toward Colonial Freedom*, which he had started writing in America, discussed the way European financial interests used their colonies as a source of raw material, as a new market for manufactured goods, and as a field for the investment of surplus capital, all without concern as to the effect of their policies on the native population and their countries. He was not the first to make such an analysis of the colonial system. Liberal Western economists had been doing so for years. However, their writings were mostly read by other liberals. Nkrumah was trying to reach an entirely new audience.

With some difficulty, he and the other members of the secretariat scraped together enough money to start a monthly review, *The New African*. The first issue appeared in March 1946 with the subtitle, "The Voice of the Awakened African" and the motto, "For Unity and Absolute Independence."

"Unity" meant to Nkrumah at this time the unity of all West Africa, not only the four British colonies of Nigeria, Ghana, Sierra Leone, and tiny Gambia, but the more numerous French West African colonies as well. Although the French claimed that their colonial peoples were full French citizens, in actual practice Africans in French territories were paid as little and exploited as badly as Africans elsewhere. Only a privileged handful became deputies (the equivalent of senators in the United States) in the French Assembly.

On a trip to Paris, Nkrumah met with some of the French African deputies, among them Félix Houphouet-Boigny, a physician who would later be President of the Ivory Coast, and the poet, Léopold Senghor, future President of Senegal. Senghor and a few other French Africans accepted Nkrumah's invitation to attend a West African Conference in London, organized by the secretariat. Nkrumah was greatly encouraged, seeing their co-operation as a first step toward West African unity.

The momentum of his London activities increased. He became president of the West African Students' Union and extended its operations to giving aid and advice to all West Africans living in England, including seamen stranded there after the end of the war, who were now living in direst poverty. He composed numerous memoranda to the Secretary of State for the Colonies, pointing out inequities in

British colonies and demanding action to remedy them. He wrote articles for *Pan-Africa*, a magazine of high intellectual caliber whose contributors also included George Padmore, Peter Abrahams, and Wallace Johnson.

For most young Africans, London was a stimulating place. They were mastering professions long denied their countrymen: engineering, medicine, and law. They were exploring literature and art. They were drawn together by their youth and their idealism, and above all by the challenge of helping to make Africa free. Bitterness and suspicion would break some of the friendships formed in London; nothing would ever efface the memory of those years.

Though racial discrimination existed in England, there was not the calm assumption of superiority so universal in the colonies. A large number of English people took it for granted that a person should be judged for what he was, regardless of the color of his skin. Also, the lines of segregation were less distinct than in America. For example, a black man could mount a soap box in Hyde Park and make a speech without police interference. Nkrumah took pleasure in reading the Communist paper, the *Daily Worker*, on the Underground (the British subway), to see how fellow passengers would react. It was true that they stared at him, but their expressions were amused rather than hostile.

Nkrumah made it a point to learn all he could about the various British political parties from the most radical to the most conservative, to find out how they were organized. He now called himself a Marxian Socialist. He had Communist friends and attended Communist as well as other political meetings but did not join the Communist Party. Something of Socialist or Communist theory and terminology permeated his thinking. He saw the fight against colonialism not merely as a struggle of black Africans against white Europeans, but as a class struggle of the exploited masses against their exploiters.

Once his country was free, Nkrumah envisaged a government dedicated to improving the lot of these "masses," providing them with free education, decent housing, jobs, social security, adequate medical facilities—all the things so pitifully lacking in the Gold Coast. To achieve this, he conceived the idea of forming a small secret organization, its membership limited to "persons who are trained and engaged in political revolution as a profession." He named it The Circle.

The motto of The Circle was "The Three S's—Service, Sacrifice, Suffering." Its aims were: "To maintain ourselves and The Circle as the Revolutionary Vanguard of the struggle for West African Unity and National Independence," and "to support the idea and claims of the All West African National Congress in its struggle to create and maintain a Union of African Socialist Republics."

To prove their dedication, members were expected to fast from sunrise to sunset on the twenty-first of each month and to meditate daily on "the cause The Circle stands for." They were pledged to avoid the use of violence "except as a last resort," to obey irrevocably the commands and instructions of the Grand Council of The Circle, and to accept "the leadership of Kwame Nkrumah." Members had to take an oath of allegiance, binding them to live up to the aspirations of The Circle, never to divulge its secrets, plans or movements nor to betray a member brother or use the influence of The Circle for their "own personal interests or advertisement."

According to Peter Abrahams, Nkrumah originally proposed the idea of The Circle to Jomo Kenyatta, suggesting that each member spill a few drops of blood into a bowl and take a blood oath "of secrecy and dedication to the emancipation of Africa." Kenyatta reportedly scoffed at the idea. A man of great sophistication, he saw the struggle for African freedom in terms of the twentieth century, in which blood oaths had no part. Ironically, Kenyatta would later be accused of supporting the much more ritualistic and bloody Mau Mau movement in Kenya.

If The Circle actually became a working organization, the members stayed true to their oath of allegiance and revealed nothing. Its creed remained in Nkrumah's possession and was published in full in his autobiography.

Nkrumah knew that he could not set the Gold Coast free while he was living in London. To accomplish any of his objectives he must return home. Still he stayed on, hampered by lack of funds for his passage. He had been in London nearly two years when he received a letter from Ako Adjei, who had returned to the Gold Coast. The letter contained an interesting proposal.

Ako Adjei had recently joined a group called the United Gold Coast Convention who were urging the government to make certain reforms. The UGCC were not rushing things, but their ultimate aim was "independence in the shortest possible time." They had now come to realize that the colonial authorities would pay more attention to them if they could prove they were speaking for the Gold Coast people as a whole. Accordingly, they were on the outlook for someone who was willing to tour the country and get them new members. On Ako Adjei's recommendation they were offering the job to Nkrumah, with a salary of one hundred pounds a month—$280.00—and a car at his disposal.

From friends in London, Nkrumah learned more about the United Gold Coast Convention. Its founder and first president was a wealthy timber merchant named George A. Grant, an old-timer known as "Pa Grant," who felt that the governor was giving too much power to the chiefs and was neglecting the needs of businessmen like himself. The UGCC members were mostly from the Coastal Elite, fairly wealthy, educated abroad, and completely Europeanized.

Even without knowing them personally, Nkrumah sensed
that what they meant by independence was simply changing
the white government for a black government, with the
same structure as before. He judged they had little interest
in making life better for the average citizen.

While he was debating what to do about the offer, a letter
came from the UGCC vice-president, Dr. Joseph Boakye
Danquah, urging him to accept. Dr. Danquah was well
known both as a barrister and a scholar. He had written
several books on Akan traditions. For years he had been
active in youth and reform groups. Perhaps partly because
of Danquah's reputation and partly because he felt that the
job would give him a chance to get started at the work
he most wanted, Nkrumah sent back a letter of acceptance.
The UGCC promptly forwarded him travel expenses to come
home.

On November 15, 1947, Nkrumah left Liverpool with
Kojo Botsio, his closest London friend. An Oxford graduate,
and a fellow founder of the West African National Secretariat, Botsio was returning to the Gold Coast to teach.
They sailed together as far as Freetown, Sierra Leone,
where Nkrumah stopped off to visit friends. He made two
highly applauded speeches there, one to a group of students
and the other at a public gathering. His subject on both
occasions was the need of West African colonies to unite
in a fight for independence.

Nkrumah made a second stop at Monrovia, capital of
Liberia. Monrovia had been founded by freed American
slaves when James Monroe was President of the United
States. It had been a republic since 1847 and was still the
only independent country south of the Sahara. Nkrumah
was greatly disillusioned to find that there was as much
misery in free Liberia as there was in the colonies. President
William Tubman, whom he had met, was away, but he
spoke to several government officials about a plan for hold-

ing a West African conference in Africa. The Liberians were polite but unenthusiastic. He gathered that they felt it was unfitting for an independent country to send delegates to a conference of colonial countries.

The West African Conference was not held, partly because of lack of support from other colonies and partly because Nkrumah became too busy to give it his full attention.

His funds having run short, Nkrumah made the last lap of his journey as a deck passenger—sleeping on the deck of the ship and eating food he brought with him. The African customs inspector at Takoradi looked at his passport and told him to come with him. For a moment Nkrumah feared that the authorities had decided to detain him. On the contrary, once they were alone, the customs man offered his hand and said that people had heard he was coming to help them and were eagerly awaiting his arrival.

5

GOLD COAST ORGANIZER

The art of oratory is in West Africa carried to a remarkable pitch of perfection.
—R. A. FREEMAN, *Journey to Ashanti*, 1888

Nkrumah spent the first two weeks after his return at the little gold-mining town of Tarkwa near the coast. A friend brought his mother up from Nkroful to see him. She looked frail and small and her hair had turned gray, but she had retained her air of quiet dignity. At first she looked at him doubtfully, unsure that this well-dressed man was her son. When she finally realized it was he, she began to cry.

Nkrumah made a telephone call to the United Gold Coast Convention but did not let anyone else know he was back. He wanted a little time to think, to plan, to get caught up on events in his absence.

The mood of the country had changed since he left. There was a great deal of unrest. The returned veterans of the Second World War were partially responsible. Having fought beside white soldiers to free their countries from oppression, they were unwilling to accept the status of second-class citizens again, with inferior jobs and pensions. People were also discontented because of the high prices of imported consumer goods, on which the population had learned to depend. Goods had been scarce and prices had soared during the war years. Now that the war was over, the situation was no better.

In an attempt to placate the population, the governor, Sir Alan Burns, had introduced a new constitution in 1946. This allowed most of the Legislative Council to be Africans, but still as non-official members who could criticize government policy but not change it. Burns assured the home government in London that people were "really happy and really satisfied with the new Constitution." He could not have been more mistaken. Nkrumah was only one of many knowledgeable Africans who realized that the concessions of the Burns Constitution were meaningless.

Early in January 1948, Nkrumah went to the UGCC headquarters at Saltpond on the coast and met Danquah and others of the executive committee. On the plea of poverty, they cut down heavily on his promised salary. The car they offered him proved to be a broken-down wreck. When Nkrumah accepted their terms cheerfully, he was officially inducted as general secretary.

He gave his first speech for the UGCC in Tarkwa before an audience of miners, peasants, fishermen, and other working-class people. After describing his experiences abroad, he talked of the hard struggle ahead if the Gold Coast was to become free. If they had been sleeping before, he said, now was the time to wake up. The response was enthusiastic. One elderly miner got up, pointed at Nkrumah, and said: "This young man is God's greatest gift to the Gold Coast; hear ye him!"

Back in Saltpond, Nkrumah rented an office, hired a typist, and then called a meeting of the UGCC executive committee. He had ready a detailed program of action for their consideration.

The first part of the program dealt with things to be undertaken immediately. They should form a shadow cabinet, whose members would study British administrative techniques, so as to prepare themselves to take over the government smoothly when independence came. They should enlarge their organization to enlist the support of trade unions, native societies, co-operatives, and farmers' organizations. Existing branches of the UGCC should be consolidated and new branches formed throughout the country. (According to their books, the UGCC had thirteen branches. In reality there were two, both inactive.) The chief of each town should be invited to become a patron of the local UGCC branch. Each branch should open week-end schools to educate people in self-government.

The second part of the program dealt with the long-range phase of their work. It would involve demonstrations across the country to show that the UGCC was strong enough to put pressure on the government for independence. Then the UGCC would draw up a new constitution.

Some of the committee members apparently thought Nkrumah was going too fast, but in principle they approved his entire program. Until now they had held meetings and written stirring articles about freedom, but that was the extent of it. Most of them were too occupied with their own lucrative businesses or professions to devote more than part time to UGCC activities. Now that they had a full-time paid organizer, they were willing to give him a chance.

In the next weeks, Nkrumah journeyed across the Gold Coast. He made hundreds of speeches, in Kumasi, capital of Ashanti; in Tamale, capital of the Northern Territories; and in innumerable tiny rural villages. Roads were poor. His car frequently broke down. Sometimes a Mammy truck picked him up and carried him to his destination. (Mammy trucks are a Gold Coast institution; run by the indomitable Gold Coast women, they carry both cargo and passengers.) More often than not he had to walk to the nearest village to find shelter, or simply sleep out in the open bush by the side of the road.

His engaging manner won him friends everywhere. Country people were astounded. On the whole educated Africans were arrogant and considered themselves superior to their fellow villagers. Nkrumah, on the contrary, was not too proud to sit down and share a meal in the poorest dwelling. Indeed he undoubtedly felt more comfortable with the villagers than he did with his colleagues at the UGCC.

As his reputation spread, crowds gathered in advance to wait for him. They escorted him into their villages and followed him with tears and wailing when he left. He spoke to the very poor and illiterate, for whom life was a struggle for survival, to underpaid workers, to those who had painfully acquired a little education but were still helpless to better their lot, to youths who felt they were without a future, and to women, who, in spite of their abilities and their intelligence, were the most neglected group of all under colonial rule.

It was Nkrumah's special gift that he made all these people feel important, gave them a chance to do something to help their country, and provided them with an emotional outlet. At meeting after meeting, he was greeted with applause and cheers. People crowded up afterward to sign membership cards and pay dues. The UGCC executive committee was delighted with their paid organizer. Dr. Danquah allegedly said—though he later denied it—that if everyone else failed him, he could always count on Kwame Nkrumah.

A boycott of European goods had been going on since early January. It had been organized by a progressive chief of the Brong people named Nii Bonne, in the name of the Anti-Inflation Committee. People had needed no urging to stop buying from stores they felt were overcharging them; the boycott was highly successful. Distressed merchants and government officials called in Nii Bonne to talk matters over. They agreed that if he would call off the boycott on February 28, prices would be reduced.

Also on February 28, an unarmed delegation from the Ex-Servicemen's Union marched toward Christiansborg Castle, with the intention of presenting the new governor, Sir Gerald Creasey, with a petition of their grievances. En route the police fired on them, killing a former army sergeant and wounding other veterans.

Rumors of the shooting reached Accra, where shoppers were already discovering to their disgust that prices were as high as ever. Looting broke out in European and Lebanese stores. Some buildings were set afire. The rioting spread to other towns. Before it was over, 137 people were killed and there was enormous property damage. The government declared a state of emergency. Governor Creasey announced over the radio that the trouble was the result of a Communist conspiracy and that the leaders had been arrested.

On the day the riots started in Accra, Nkrumah and Danquah were holding a rally at a town about sixty miles distant. They rushed back to Accra and arrived while the looting and burning were still going on. That night the UGCC executives held a special meeting at Dr. Danquah's house.

Dr. Danquah, a master of English prose, wrote a description of that meeting—how their "noble band" met "on that fatal night of the 28th February 1948 when Accra was burning and the imperialist agents had spilt the blood of men of Ghana," how they "sat together on a verandah" and planned "to take advantage of that day's tragic incidences and use that advantage as a fulcrum or lever for the liberation of Ghana."

The riots and violence, though not even indirectly related to UGCC activities, had put the government in an embarrassing position in which they might listen to UGCC demands. With the agreement of the committee, Nkrumah sent a telegram to Arthur Creech Jones, Secretary of State for the Colonies in London, denouncing the unprovoked attack on the veterans and the subsequent looting, burning

and killing, stating that people were demanding self-government immediately, and urging that the governor be recalled
and that a commission be sent to supervise formation of a
constituent assembly.

In Saltpond a couple of weeks later, Nkrumah was awakened by the police in the middle of the night. They searched
his room and seized the creed of his secret organization,
The Circle, and an unsigned Communist Party card. The
police officer in charge then asked him if he was a Communist. He denied it but said that in England he had as-
sociated with all parties from right to left, so that he could
learn how to organize his own nationalist party. The officer
ordered him to come with them. On Nkrumah's insistence
he produced a warrant, dated March 12, 1948, and signed
by Governor Creasey, for his arrest and detention.

He was taken to the Accra airport in a police van. Five
other UGCC leaders were already there: Dr. Danquah; Ako
Adjei; Obetsebi Lamptey, a prominent and wealthy lawyer
who like Ako Adjei was a Ga; Eric Akufo Addo, also a lawyer
and one of the best on the Gold Coast; and his brother-
in-law, the witty and eloquent William Ofori Atta, whose
leftist leanings made him more sympathetic to Nkrumah than
any of the others. They, too, had been dragged out of bed
and arrested. Apparently they were Governor Creasey's
choice for the members of the "Communist Conspiracy" he
had described to his radio audience.

These "Big Six" of the UGCC, as they were known, were
all well-to-do, except Nkrumah. Three of them had high
tribal connections. Dr. Danquah was a brother of the late
Nana Sir Ofori Atta I, chief of the Akim Abuakwa people
and the first Gold Coast African to be knighted. William
Ofori Atta was the son of the old chief, and Eric Akufo
Addo had married his daughter. They were the aristocracy
of African society, the equivalent of England's nobility.

All six were flown to Kumasi, where they spent three days

in the same jail cell. It was a good chance to work out the
details of their shadow cabinet and the form of their country's future constitution. But their discussions broke down in
a string of reproaches against Nkrumah, whom they blamed
for their humiliating plight. As long as the UGCC had
limited themselves to fine phrases about freedom, the
government had let them alone. None had realized that if
they turned their words into action, the government would
clamp down on them. Only Nkrumah accepted their situation
as inevitable. He knew from his reading that autocratic
governments never yielded power willingly.

Because of a rumor that a group of Ashanti youths, under
a new recruit to the UGCC, Krobo Edusei, were planning
to storm the prison and release their leaders, the six men
were transferred in the middle of the night to Tamale, in the
Northern Territories. There they were separated. For the
next six weeks Nkrumah was confined to a small hut and
kept under police guard.

At the end of that time all six of them were flown back
to Accra and held in the Accra airport hotel. A lawyer hired
by the UGCC, Dingle Foot, visited them there. He told
them that a Commission of Inquiry, headed by Aiken Watson, had been sent from England to investigate the causes
of the February disturbances. The prisoners had been
brought back to give testimony.

Before interviewing them, the Watson Commission insisted that they all be released. In the eight weeks they had
been held, they had not been able to see a lawyer until the
appearance of Dingle Foot. There had been no trial nor
had formal charges been made against them.

The commission called each man in separately. When
Nkrumah was summoned, the commission members showed
far more interest in his political leanings than in his
knowledge of the riots. In their final report, they stated:
". . . Mr. Nkrumah has not really departed one jot from his

avowed aim for a Union of West African Soviet Socialist Republics." It was true that Nkrumah had advocated a "Union of West African Socialist Republics." The inclusion of the word "Soviet" was invention on the part of the commission.

But the Watson Commission did one constructive thing. They dismissed the 1946 Burns Constitution as outmoded and recommended that a more democratic constitution be drafted by the Africans themselves.

After the hearings, Nkrumah returned to Saltpond and rented a new office. His first concern was a group of secondary school students who had been expelled for holding a sympathy strike on behalf of the imprisoned UGCC leaders. In Cape Coast, he opened a school for ten of them in a hired hall, with desks and benches made from kerosene tins, packing cases, and boards. Three teachers who had been dismissed for supporting the students offered their services.

At the opening ceremony on July 20, Nkrumah told the students and teachers that great things often have small beginnings and that Tuskegee Institute in Alabama, founded by Booker T. Washington in 1881 for black Americans, had begun with one student and now had thousands. His speech marked the inauguration of Ghana National College, which would have over 230 students within a year and 1,000 on the waiting list.

The UGCC executive committee had grown even cooler toward Nkrumah since the Watson Commission inquiry. While he was away at a rally, they went through his office files and seized all letters using the word "comrade," apparently equating that with communism. On September 3, he was called before the executive committee and accused of founding Ghana National College without their authority. He was demoted from the post of general secretary to UGCC treasurer.

With or without UGCC authority, Nkrumah went on

with another project, a newspaper called the Accra *Evening News,* the first issue of which appeared the day of his demotion. The daily editorial and feature articles dealt with the wrongs of the colonial system and the impending struggle for freedom. A columnist called "Rambler" expounded on the worst abuses of the colonial administration and named those he held responsible. Everyone wanted to know who "Rambler" was. If it was Nkrumah himself, he never admitted it. The *Evening News* was sensationalistic journalism, but the people loved it. Copies of this poorly printed one-page sheet were snatched up as soon as they came from the press and read aloud by the literate to the illiterate.

One after another civil officials mentioned in the paper started suits for libel. Regardless of whether or not the statements about them were true, they always won. Again and again, Nkrumah's friends raised money to pay off the claimants. Some insisted the suits were instigated by the government to bankrupt the *Evening News,* but if so they failed badly. It is said that at this time the government realized that Nkrumah, far from being ruined by the "Communist" label they had pinned on him, had become a formidable opponent.

Increasingly Nkrumah concentrated on youth. He organized a Youth Study Group in Accra, the Ghana Youth Association in Sekondi, and the Ashanti Youth Association, then united all three as the Committee on Youth Organization. Most of the members also belonged to the UGCC, but the UGCC aim of "self-government within the shortest possible time" had little appeal for them. Nkrumah proposed an alternate slogan: "Self-government now!" The young people happily painted it on walls and buildings everywhere.

In December, the government at last decided to follow the recommendation of the Watson Commission and nominated a committee composed of forty African members under the chairmanship of Justice Henley Coussey, to work

out a new constitution. As expected, the nominees were
chiefs or Coastal Elite. Trade unions, farmers, and small
traders were not represented. Dr. Danquah and four other
UGCC members were nominated; Nkrumah and Ako Adjei
were excluded.

At a massive rally in Accra, Nkrumah outlined his own
recommendations to the Coussey Committee: universal
adult suffrage instead of suffrage for taxpayers and property owners; a national assembly elected by the people; a
cabinet responsible to the assembly. The national assembly
he proposed was modeled after the British Parliament and
was similar to the French National Assembly and the United
States Congress. Only in the colonies would these ideas have
been considered revolutionary. One newspaperman commented that each of the 25,000 words in Nkrumah's ninety-
minute speech was "a nail in the coffin of colonialism and
imperialism."

All during the spring of 1949, Nkrumah continued his
cross-country speeches, meeting with ever greater enthusiasm. The UGCC executive committee made it clear that
they now wanted to get rid of him, subjecting him to a
series of petty persecutions and harassments. Two of his
supporters, Kojo Botsio, his friend of the London days, and
Komla Gbedemah, head of the Ghana Youth Association,
felt it was time to break away from the parent organization
and form their own party. The idea had certainly occurred
to Nkrumah long before. In his opinion, the UGCC leadership were self-centered individuals anxious only for political
power.

With Kojo Botsio, Gbedemah, and a few others he trusted,
he drew up plans for the new party, one that would follow
the wishes of the masses, not dictate to them. They named
it the Convention People's Party. Nkrumah insisted that the
word "Convention" be in the name, so people would know

that it was an outgrowth of the United Gold Coast Convention.

On Sunday, June 12, 1949, some sixty thousand people crowded the Accra Arena, the largest rally in Gold Coast history. Although it was the rainy season, the sun shone brightly. With the skill of an actor, Nkrumah described the struggle he had had with the UGCC since his return. He paced back and forth across the platform, using gestures to emphasize each point. Sometimes he shook his head sadly at some monstrous failing of his opponents. Or he would turn to the audience with a captivating smile, seeming to address each one personally.

At the end, he said quietly that he was faced with three major questions. Should he, at this stage of the political struggle, pack up and leave?

"No!" shouted the crowd.

Or should he remain—and keep his mouth shut?

Again, "No!"

Then he asked if they felt he might break away from "a faltering and quailing leadership" and throw in his lot with the chiefs and the people for "full self-government now"?

The cries of approval and the applause were thunderous.

It was in this emotion-charged atmosphere that Kwame Nkrumah announced the birth of the Convention People's Party.

6

POSITIVE ACTION

Nothing must be left to chance and there is no room for
complacency.

—NKRUMAH

Four days after Nkrumah announced his new party, the
UGCC held its own open meeting at the Accra Palladium.
One of the speakers was the wealthy Ga lawyer, Obetsebi
Lamptey, who asked the other Ga people in the audience
why they had let themselves be led by "a stranger"—a man
from Nzima. His appeal to tribal loyalties fell flat. The crowd
hissed him.

Two or three of the UGCC leaders tentatively approached
Nkrumah and suggested a compromise. Would he come
back if he were reinstated as general secretary and if his
CPP were incorporated into the UGCC as a vanguard
group? Nkrumah replied that he did not like splitting the
ranks of Gold Coast nationalists any more than they did,
but that he could consider their proposal only if they would
elect a new executive committee which would carry out the
policies people were demanding. After waiting a few days
and hearing nothing further, he formally tendered his resignation.

Ako Adjei and a few other members of the UGCC would
later join him, for shorter or longer periods. Others, Dr.
Danquah and Obetsebi Lamptey among them, became his
implacable enemies. With some justice they claimed that in

return for their kindness in giving him a job when he was penniless and unknown, he had undermined their authority. They also accused him of turning the people away from them. The UGCC members derisively dubbed the CPP "Verandah Boys," the name for the unemployed who haunted hotels and streets looking for odd jobs.

Nkrumah was too occupied with the CPP to pay much attention to these attacks, which was perhaps a mistake. A central committee was chosen. Kojo Botsio became CPP secretary. Nkrumah was chairman. Komla Gbedemah of the Ewe people, a former science master in a secondary school, who spoke most Gold Coast languages perfectly; N. A. Welbeck; Kwesi Plange; Kofi Baako; the generous and impulsive Krobo Edusei of the Ashanti; Dzenkle Dzewu; and Ashie Nikoe were the other members.

Although only Nkrumah and Kojo Botsio had university degrees, they were all intelligent and literate and all were devoted to the cause of freedom.

The executive committee drew up a six-point program: 1) to fight for full self-government by all constitutional means; 2) to serve as a political vanguard to stop oppression and establish a democratic government; 3) to secure and maintain unity between chiefs and people; 4) to improve conditions for working people in co-operation with trade unions; 5) to work for the reconstruction of their country to make it a place where a free people would govern themselves; 6) to assist in the creation of a united and self-governing West Africa.

Once free from the restrictions of the UGCC, Nkrumah began a national campaign on a grand scale. Vans with loudspeakers spread the CPP platform throughout the country. Full-time political workers were hired, one of their tasks being to give political lectures and educate the people in self-government.

The UGCC branches Nkrumah had established in remote

areas proved more than willing to transfer their allegiance to the CPP. After all, Nkrumah was the only UGCC leader who had deigned to visit them, to talk to them, to sit down and eat with them.

The CPP adopted "Freedom!" as their rally cry. Their motto was "Forward Ever, Backward Never!" The CPP salutation was the Freedom Sign, the right hand raised, palm forward and fingers outstretched. Red, white, and green were the Party's colors. European firms, seeing a quick profit, imported caps, shirts, and dress material in these colors. There was also an "Nkrumah cloth," with the imprint of his portrait. Men wore shirts of Nkrumah cloth; women used it for their wraparound skirts.

A large part of Nkrumah's support came from women. They were his chief field organizers and in advance of a scheduled speech they traveled ahead to make preparations. In their enthusiasm they sometimes went to extremes. A Kumasi woman ended her fiery speech by slashing her face with a knife and smearing blood over herself. Then she challenged the men to do the same to show that no sacrifice was too great in the struggle for freedom.

The CPP was organized on democratic lines. Nkrumah submitted his ideas to the central committee for approval. The committee in turn submitted all resolutions for the consideration of CPP representatives of the four Gold Coast territories. In actual practice all Nkrumah's proposals were accepted unanimously.

If people did not know what to believe, they asked Nkrumah. He informed them that what they should hope for was a new society which would give them good jobs and education for their children. He told them that these things would come only with work and suffering. And by following Nkrumah.

Myths about Nkrumah spread. "Nkrumah will never die," people said. Bullets, they said, could not touch him. He was compared to Christ, the Messiah. People began to call him Osagyefo, the Redeemer.

In October 1949, the Coussey Committee published its long-awaited recommendations for a new constitution. The committee recommended franchise for all taxpayers (not universal adult suffrage as Nkrumah had demanded) and wider African representation in the Legislative Council, but with little more power than before. Although Nkrumah had expected no more, he was shocked that this all-African committee had not even recommended self-government.

On November 20, he voiced his objections at a meeting of the Ghana People's Representatives, to which more than fifty organizations had been invited to send delegates. His words had their usual magic. The assembly resolved that the Coussey report was unacceptable and demanded that the Gold Coast be granted self-government at once.

On December 15, Nkrumah wrote the new governor, Sir Charles Arden-Clarke, that if the government continued to ignore the legitimate aspirations of the people, as outlined in the proposed amendments to the Coussey report, then the Convention People's Party would embark on Positive Action and continue until their demands were accepted. The lead article in that day's Accra *Evening News* carried the headline, "The Era of Positive Action Draws Nigh." At a CPP meeting held in the Accra Arena that night, Nkrumah announced that if there was no response from the government by January 1, 1950, Positive Action would be declared soon after that.

Nkrumah had frequently spoken of Positive Action, a term he had first heard in connection with Gandhi's passive resistance campaign. He wrote a pamphlet to explain just what it meant—putting pressure on the British by all legitimate and constitutional means—newspaper and educational campaigns, demonstrations, strikes and boycotts. He had often stressed that Positive Action did not mean violence.

Nonetheless the colonial government was frightened by those two words.

The Colonial Secretary, R. H. Saloway, sent for Nkrumah. Accompanied as usual by several CPP colleagues, he went to the Secretary's office. Saloway, a suave and polished Britisher, spoke to him sternly as to a recalcitrant schoolboy. He must not be so rash as to start Positive Action, Saloway said. It could only mean chaos. Moreover, it would not work here as it had in India. Africans could not endure pain and privation, as Indians had: "Mark my words, my good man, within three days the people here will let you down."

Nkrumah stood firm. On January 8, when no further word had come from the government, he announced that Positive Action would begin at midnight with a general strike to include everyone but hospital employees, police, and those in essential public utilities. He stressed that there must be no burning, looting, rioting, or violence of any kind.

The government took action the next day by broadcasting that Positive Action was over and that people should go back to work "like their brothers in other areas." Nkrumah, learning that a few Accra stores had opened, called an emergency meeting at the Arena and talked for two hours. From then on, all stores remained closed. Trains stayed in the depots. Government services were shut down. Workers stayed home. A visitor in Accra during those days reported that it was like a dead city. It was the same elsewhere.

The Joint Provincial Council of Chiefs invited the CPP leaders to meet with them at Dodowah, their headquarters, to discuss a peaceful settlement. Nkrumah arrived with three other central committee members. Politely and firmly, he told the chiefs that Positive Action must continue until the CPP demands were met. Each chief spoke in turn. Without exception they abused him for what he was doing.

In a speech in Accra, Nkrumah reported his meeting with the chiefs. He was angry. If the chiefs would not co-operate with the people in their struggle for freedom, he said, a day might come when they would run away and leave their sandals behind them. The comment was a grave insult and was later quoted as proof that Nkrumah had always intended to get rid of the chiefs. This was not accurate. Nkrumah had a deep respect for African traditions and felt that the chiefs had a place as the spiritual leaders of the people. What he resented was their support of colonial rule.

With the chiefs behind them, the government took more drastic action. A state of emergency was declared and a curfew was imposed. The Accra *Evening News* and two other newspapers the CPP supported, the Sekondi *Morning Telegram* and the Cape Coast *Daily Mail,* were banned. Their editors were arrested. Police raided the CPP headquarters and confiscated books and papers. Kojo Botsio, the CPP secretary, was arrested on January 15; other CPP leaders were arrested in the next several days.

In Accra, Syrian and Lebanese merchants and British civilians were made into special constables and given police clubs. Some of them took the law into their own hands and beat up Africans at random. Thus, although violence did occur during Positive Action, it was at the instigation of the authorities, not the CPP.

At a meeting of the Legislative Council on January 20, one of the chiefly members, Nana Sir Tsibu Darku, made a motion deploring "the intimidations of those who have set their hearts upon the disruption of the country's peace and security" and supporting "the emergency measures taken by the government to prevent further outbreaks of violence." His motion was supported by other African members of the council, including Dr. Danquah, vice-president of the UGCC.

The next day, Nkrumah walked to the Accra CPP headquarters after a day's absence from the city. As he approached it, he saw police guarding the entrance. One of the officers came over to him and told him that he was under arrest. He went without protest. In the police van he heard over the radio the news of his own arrest. All was now quiet at the scene, the commentator announced.

Nkrumah's first trial lasted about a week. The CPP brought in two English barristers to defend him, though Nkrumah knew in advance that it would be useless. The charge against him was that he had incited others to take part in an illegal strike. He was given two separate sentences of one year each.

He was then handcuffed and taken to Cape Coast for a second trial on the charge of sedition. This was in connection with an article in the Cape Coast *Daily Mail*, headlined "A Campaign of Lies," denouncing the government for broadcasting that Positive Action was over, for which the paper's editor, Kofi Baako, had already been sent to jail. As the publisher of the paper, Nkrumah was also found guilty and sentenced to another year. His three years were to run consecutively.

Back in Accra, he was taken to James Fort Prison. Originally James Fort had been built by the Company of Royal Adventurers of England Trading to Africa and had been used as their headquarters while they were expanding the West African slave trade. As Nkrumah was waiting to be locked up, he was able to talk for a few minutes with Komla Gbedemah of the CPP central committee, who was just being released. Nkrumah was fond of this big young man with an engaging smile and a hearty scorn for colonial rulers. To Gbedemah, he gave full responsibility for handling CPP affairs and seeing that the Accra *Evening News* resumed publishing.

In Europe it was customary to grant favored treatment to political prisoners, condemned not for crimes but because of their principles. At Fort James, there were no such distinctions. Political prisoners shared the same lot as criminals. Nkrumah was brought to a cell that already held ten of his CPP friends. Conditions were unsanitary, and the food was so revolting that his colleagues had gone on a hunger strike. Nkrumah insisted that they eat, arguing that they had to keep healthy so that they would have the strength for the work awaiting them when they were released.

After a brief exercise period each morning, the men were assigned to weave fishnets or prepare reeds for basket making. At four in the afternoon they were locked up for the night. Newspapers were forbidden. They could write one letter a month but could not keep pencils or paper.

Somehow Nkrumah got hold of a stubby pencil. At night, while the others slept, he wrote instructions for the party on toilet paper. He folded the sheets in tiny packages, and in a manner never revealed, got them to Komla Gbedemah. Because of these regularly delivered messages, a rumor spread among the superstitious that Nkrumah left his cell each night in the form of a white cat.

The government had won the first round. Deprived of its leadership, the campaign of Positive Action died down. But Nkrumah knew that he had not been forgotten. Crowds often gathered outside the prison, singing hymns interspersed with party songs. Their favorite, sung to the tune of "John Brown's Body," was:

> Kwame Nkrumah's body lies a-moldering in his cell
> But his work goes prospering on.

On Sundays, prisoners were allowed to attend church services and had more time in the prison yard. This gave Nkrumah and his cellmates a chance to talk with the other political prisoners interned at Fort James. Under the eyes of their guards, they formed a committee and elected two subcommittees. One was headed by Kojo Botsio, the other by an ex-serviceman arrested during Positive Action.

Executions took place on an average of once a month, usually for crimes of passion. The prisoners knew when there was to be a hanging because they were locked in an upper room. When they passed the gallows later, on their way to the washrooms, they occasionally saw a few bloodstains, the only evidence that a human life had been taken.

Nkrumah had long opposed the death penalty. He believed that people were what the society in which they lived made them. The death penalty, he felt, solved nothing. His convictions were reinforced by the horror of these executions. During the long, monotonous prison days, he had time to reflect about such things. It seemed to him that crime, per se, was a European import. Before the white men came, tribal taboos usually curbed wrongdoing, and bribery and corruption were unknown. He could not deny what was good in European civilization, but in prison he saw more clearly than ever the spiritual harm that white occupation had done in Africa.

Somehow the months passed. With his stub of a pencil Nkrumah wrote the party song, beginning, "There shall be victory for us." His supporters sang it for him from outside the prison walls. In June 1950, he learned that Kwesi Plange of the CPP central committee had won a Cape Coast by-election to the Legislative Council, thus becoming the first CPP member. Kojo Botsio, who had supported Nkrumah faithfully since their days in London together, was released. Nkrumah wrote him a farewell note, expressing gratitude for his support and urging him to help keep their forces together.

There were days when Nkrumah's cellmates grew despondent and bitter. It is unlikely that Nkrumah himself was always cheerful, but he did what he could to keep up morale. It was unrealistic to believe that the British would grant them freedom on a silver platter, he reminded his fellow inmates. Prison was an inevitable part of the struggle for independence. They had to prove that they were patient, that they were strong and that they could not be discouraged.

7

PRISON TO PRIME MINISTER

The worst of some days is the best of others.

—African proverb

When Nkrumah had been in prison about a year, the government announced the terms of a new constitution, based on the Coussey Committee recommendations. The Executive Council would now include eight Africans in addition to three Europeans nominated by the governor. The Legislative Council would be replaced by a Legislative Assembly of 84 members, 75 elected and nine nominated by the governor. Of the 75, 38 would be elected directly by town voters and indirectly by rural voters. The other 37 were to be chosen by the Provincial Councils of Chiefs. Suffrage was still limited to taxpayers, but the voting age was reduced from 25 to 21, largely because of an eloquent plea from the one CPP Legislative Council member, Kwesi Plange.

For the elective assembly seats, the first general election in Gold Coast history was called on February 8, 1951. Nkrumah still felt the reforms in the constitution did not go far enough, but he knew it was vitally important for the CPP to show its strength in the election. Accordingly, CPP candidates were registered on the rolls of all election districts.

Nkrumah barely qualified as a candidate himself. By Gold Coast law, no one who had been sentenced to prison for more than one year could run for office, but since Nkrumah's three-year sentence was divided into three terms of one year each, he was technically eligible. Even so, there was considerable opposition to his candidacy. Gbedemah finally got his forms completed and submitted, in Accra Central, the district of Nkrumah's choice, just a few minutes before the registration period closed.

Nkrumah directed the election campaign as best he could from prison. Gbedemah and other party leaders who were still free, stumped the country, urging people to vote and telling them how to vote. They traveled thousands of miles each week and made an average of seven to eight speeches a day. Everywhere they impressed upon their audiences that Kwame Nkrumah was their leader and that he was in prison for them. It turned out that the government, by arresting Nkrumah, had done the party a favor. He became a martyr. Among Africans, there was no stigma attached to being jailed by the white authorities. It was obvious to all that if the government had not feared Nkrumah, they would have let him alone.

At four o'clock the morning after election night, the warden came and told Nkrumah that he had won in the Accra district. His fellow prisoners were delighted and even the guards seemed pleased. The final returns showed that he had received a personal vote of 22,780 out of a possible 23,122.

The Convention People's Party won 34 of the 38 elected seats in the Legislative Assembly, 29 in the rural areas and five in the cities. The UGCC won only three assembly seats; two of these were occupied by Dr. Danquah and William Ofori Atta, the man whom Nkrumah had always considered as the most liberal of the "Big Six." A newcomer to politics was Dr. Kofi Busia of Ashanti, a sociology professor and brother of a tribal chief. Defeated by the electorate as an Independent, he was granted a seat by the chiefs. Busia seems early to have taken a dislike to Nkrumah, whom he loftily dismissed as "a demagogue of inferior intellect." Most of the 37 members chosen by the councils of chiefs were conservative as were the 9 Europeans appointed by the governor. In spite of its success in the election, the CPP was a minority in the Council. Nonetheless there could be no doubt in anyone's mind that they were the choice of the Gold Coast people.

The government had not expected such a landslide victory, but Governor Sir Charles Arden-Clarke accepted the situation as inevitable. Since henceforth he would have to work with Nkrumah, he decided to do it as gracefully as he could. On February 12, four days after the election, he ordered Nkrumah's release. The prison superintendent came to his cell and told him to be ready to leave within the hour. He had little packing to do. Even his precious pencil stub had no further value except as a souvenir. Four other political prisoners were granted a reprieve at the same time.

As the prison gate opened to let them out, they were greeted by a mammoth crowd, cheering, shouting, waving, and singing party songs. There were market women with white paint on their faces to signify victory, clerks, workers, schoolchildren—a large percentage of Accra's African population. Nkrumah, wearing a green shirt open at the neck, was lifted shoulder high and carried to an open car. Through crowds which grew increasingly dense, they moved slowly toward the Arena. A trip that usually took fifteen minutes lasted more than two hours.

At the Arena, before the cheering audience, Nkrumah participated in a ceremony which called for a sheep to be slaughtered. Nkrumah stepped into its blood seven times, a rite intended to cleanse him of the contamination of prison. From then on he and his prison comrades often wore a peaked white hat with the two letters "P.G." embroidered on it. The initials stood for "Prison Graduate."

One CPP member, Archie Casely-Hayford, had escaped

arrest because of his distinguished background. He was a Cambridge graduate who since 1947 had served the Gold Coast as a senior magistrate. His grandfather, Reverend Joseph Hayford had been in the cabinet of the Fanti Confederation, and his father, Joseph Casely-Hayford, was a political leader and social reformer. A member of the UGCC, Archie Casely-Hayford's revolutionary heritage had led him to switch to the CPP at the time of the split. On the platform with the CPP "Prison Graduates," he wore an old-fashioned nightcap embroidered with the initials "D.V.B." —"Defender of the Veranda Boys."

The day after his release, Nkrumah reported to Christiansborg Castle, at the invitation of Governor Arden-Clarke. "A tall, broadshouldered man, sun-tanned, with an expression of firmness and discipline but with a twinkle of kindness in his eyes," he described this representative of "British imperialism." The governor seems to have been equally favorably impressed. The "rabble rouser" he had expected turned out to be intelligent, reasonable, and sincere.

Nkrumah said at once that he would always be frank with the governor, that only in this way could they build mutual trust and confidence. Sir Charles agreed. From then on they worked together in a harmony that surprised everyone.

The governor told Nkrumah that his title would now be Leader of Government Business and that his duties would be similar to those of a British Prime Minister, except that his decisions would need the approval of the British Crown, which the governor represented. His first task would be to form a government—that is to nominate the seven Africans who, with himself and the three Europeans the governor appointed, would make up a cabinet, replacing the former Executive Council.

Literally overnight Nkrumah was transformed from a prisoner to one of the top leaders of the land. The Director of James Fort prison, hearing the news, offered his resignation. "I am not prepared to take orders from one of my former inmates," he said. Nkrumah himself took his dazzling rise calmly. That afternoon he agreed to a press conference with foreign journalists who had come to the Gold Coast to cover the election.

He told them that he had come out of jail into the Assembly with no bitterness toward Britain. What he wanted for the Gold Coast was independence with the status of membership in the British Commonwealth. He opposed racial discrimination in any form, just as he opposed imperialism. As for the new constitution, it was "bogus and fraudulent," as he had said before, since it gave African ministers portfolios but no real power. Still, he felt it would be to his country's advantage to give it a trial and thereby prove its contradictions.

After conferring with the CPP central committee, he submitted to the governor his nominations for the seven cabinet ministers. Five of them were CPP leaders: Kojo Botsio, Minister of Education and Social Welfare; Komla Gbedemah, Minister of Health and Labor; Archie Casely-Hayford, Minister of Agriculture and Natural Resources; T. Hutton Mills, Minister of Commerce, Industry and Mines; Dr. Ansah Koi, Minister of Communications and Works.

He did not offer cabinet posts to Dr. Danquah or William Ofori Atta. Though their education and abilities made them eligible, he did not trust them. He did offer a post to Dr. Kofi Busia, the Independent from Ashanti, but Busia declined. The remaining two posts went to chiefs: E. O. Assafu-Adjaye of the Ashanti, and Kabachewura J. A. Braimah from the Northern Territories, as Minister of Local Government and Minister Without Portfolio. It did not escape Nkrumah's attention that the three cabinet posts given to Europeans appointed by the governor were the most important: Minister of Finance, Minister of Defence and External Affairs, and Minister of Justice and Attorney General.

Members of the UGCC, who had once attacked Nkrumah for demanding self-government too soon, now accused him and the CPP of giving up their principles because they had titles and good jobs. Nkrumah struck back by suggesting that if these men wanted "Self-Government Now," they should join the CPP and continue Positive Action. No one accepted his challenge. He had been sure they would not. He was equally sure that if he had refused to work with the government, they would have criticized him for being afraid to accept responsibility.

The new Legislative Assembly met for the first time on February 20. For the post of Speaker, Nkrumah nominated Sir Emmanuel Quist, an elderly lawyer of Accra's Ga aristocracy, who was even more conservative than the UGCC. Although he wanted the CPP to have the majority voice, Nkrumah was at this stage leaning over backward to include all shades of opinion and politics in his government.

He also wanted to make sure that those of the CPP who were so suddenly elevated in rank would not forget that they were servants of the people. The newly elected officials were urged to donate part of their salaries to the CPP, as Nkrumah did. The government offered them new modern bungalows on the hills in the outskirts of Accra, but most of them continued to live in humbler quarters in the African section.

Nkrumah himself moved into a two-story red brick building in the heart of Accra, more modest than the villas of many lesser British civil servants. Except for a few security officers on guard, he might have been any ordinary middle-class citizen. He brought his mother from Nkroful to keep house for him, and in the African fashion took in a few relatives as permanent guests.

His energy astounded the British officials, who were accustomed to taking things easy. He rose at four and seldom got to bed before midnight. In addition to his government duties, he continued to be active in the CPP, of which he had been made secretary for life. All day and late into the evening there were interviews, meetings, speeches to prepare.

He was almost never alone. People flocked to his home with their problems, as they had done in former times to their chiefs. He never turned anyone away. Petitioners gathered around him when he took his first cup of tea in the morning and were there late in the afternoon, when he ate his dinner of African food, usually his only meal of the day. One day a stranger followed him to his bath, though he was discreet enough to present his request through a crack in the bathroom door. The petitioners included young men wanting work, sick people wanting to be cured, old men who wanted him to make their wives give them sons. All took for granted that he had the miraculous power to fulfill their wishes.

Nkrumah was feeling his way during those first weeks. His impromptu office was a room in the main ministry building. Here he attempted to master the intricacies of government administration for which his American college education had ill prepared him. The governor had provided him with an adviser from the Ministry of Agriculture, and he had access to other bureaus, but he was hampered at every turn in getting the information he needed. What struck him most forcefully was the utter indifference of the administrators to the needs of the country they were being paid to govern.

In the Gold Coast as in other colonial governments, the policy had been not to establish a balanced economy but to make money. Gold was mined for a profit, but almost no attempt had been made to appraise the other mineral resources of the country. About 80 per cent of the staple foods were imported, though the climate and rich soil made it possible to grow almost anything.

Whatever was right for England was considered right for the Gold Coast. English law was transferred wholesale to the Gold Coast, in spite of its difference in culture, customs and tradition. A minor example of British insularity was the matter of police uniforms. In England policemen wore woolen uniforms. Accordingly, woolen uniforms were imported for policemen in the tropical Gold Coast.

With all these handicaps, Nkrumah set up a five-year plan for economic and industrial development and actually got some projects under way. He began his battle against the Gold Coast's 90 per cent illiteracy by constructing new schools, promising himself that he would not be satisfied until education was free and compulsory for all.

Since independence was now only a matter of time, he pondered the problem of Africanization of government offices. Some 20 per cent of the government staff were now African, but nearly all were in junior posts. The recruiting and training of African civil servants had to be speeded up, but in the meantime it was essential that British civil servants be persuaded to stay on. Nkrumah knew this would not be easy, especially among the old-school colonists, who still considered it degrading to sit down next to an African. Above all, it was essential to import teachers, scientists, technicians from abroad to help out in the trying period of the first years. He hoped that most of these people would come from Great Britain. It would be simpler since English was the official language, but he resolved not to refuse technical or financial aid from any country, provided there were no strings attached.

After four months of the most arduous labor of his life, he felt a need for a change, a time to crystallize his thinking. An invitation came from Dr. Horace Mann Bond, now dean of Lincoln University, to come to America and receive an honorary doctor of laws degree. Nkrumah accepted and invited Kojo Botsio, his Minister of Education, to go with him.

On May 30, 1951, more than seven thousand people came to Accra airport to see them off. Women spread out their bright-colored cloths for Nkrumah to walk on as he headed to the plane for his first flight.

At New York's Idlewild airport (now Kennedy), a State Department protocol officer gave him an official welcome. A group of Gold Coast students had risen at dawn to meet the plane. Also present were British officials, black American leaders, a United Nations representative, and a host of reporters and photographers eager to get a story on the first African in colonial Africa south of the Sahara to win a high government post. A police escort took him to his hotel. Later that afternoon he found time to visit his former landlady in Harlem, who had taken care of him when he was starving, and to slip a hundred-dollar bill into her hand.

The next day he went to Philadelphia where the mayor gave him the golden key to the city. He must have remembered the times when he slept in railroad stations and on park benches. The day after that he was back at Lincoln University.

On the stage of the auditorium, which was packed with students and visitors, Dr. Bond presented him with an honorary doctor of laws degree. Nkrumah made an informal speech about the Convention People's Party's "arduous struggle against imperialist tactics." Afterward a number of graduates told him that they wanted to come to the Gold Coast to help. He assured them that as soon as Independence arrived, their skills would be welcome.

Journalists pursued him everywhere. He was tactful when they asked him whether he was having any difficulties working with the colonial government. He did not feel that this was the time or the place to air his differences with his British colleagues. When an Australian journalist asked him if he wore a loincloth in his own country, he pretended not to hear. What bored him most were the inevitable questions as to whether there was any Communist influence in the CPP. Patiently he replied, again and again, that in the Gold

Coast as elsewhere, the label of communism was pinned on anyone who challenged the authorities. It was a favorite "imperialist bogey."

Back in New York he conferred with United Nations Secretary General Trygve Lie, Dr. Ralph Bunche, and other UN officials. When Trygve Lie presented him to the Russian ambassador, Constantine Zwichanko, he said wryly, "I expect he is the first Moscow agent you have met."

There was a quick trip to Washington to talk with more State Department officials. Like so many other tourists, Nkrumah laid a wreathe before the Abraham Lincoln Memorial. In New York, before he left, Mayor Vincent Impellitteri gave a large dinner party in his honor. He returned to the Gold Coast, after a stopover in London, confident that he had won many new and valuable friends for his country and feeling refreshed and eager to return to work.

On June 29, a few days after his return, he announced over the radio "a new deal for cocoa." In doing so, he was risking his entire political career.

Cocoa-tree seedlings had been brought to the Gold Coast in 1879 from the island of Fernando Po by a Gold Coast African named Tetteh Quashie, who had been working on a cocoa plantation there. Cocoa trees proved an ideal crop, especially in the forest area of Ashanti. A farmer had only to clear a plot of land of small trees and undergrowth, leaving larger trees to provide shade, and plant the seedlings. From then on his main chore was to keep the undergrowth down. A tree produced pods within five years and could continue producing for twenty years.

By 1950 cocoa exports totaled 267,000 tons and sold for 54,604,000 pounds (almost $153 million), amounting to about 72 per cent of the entire Gold Coast export trade. When Western Europeans or Americans bought a chocolate bar or drank a cup of cocoa, chances were 50 per cent that they were made from Gold Coast cocoa beans.

The British had never undertaken to grow cocoa plantations. The industry was left in the hands of Africans, who raised the cocoa trees with the aid of their families or with a few hired helpers. About half the cocoa farms were run by Gold Coast women.

In recent years the cocoa industry had been menaced by the swollen shoot disease, caused by a virus carried by the mealy bug. The disease was fatal, and it spread alarmingly. The only way to halt it that agriculturists had found was to cut down and burn all infected trees. From 1946 to 1951, the colonial authorities ordered some twelve million trees destroyed. Farmers objected strenuously. A rumor spread that the British were trying to wreck the cocoa farms and the country's prosperity, so as to make the forthcoming gift of freedom worthless.

At first Nkrumah had supported the farmers against the government. He now realized that cutting down diseased trees was a necessity. The British had proved incapable of convincing the stubborn farmers. Nkrumah took over the job.

In his June 29 broadcast, he told cocoa farmers that if they did not co-operate, the entire cocoa industry would be wiped out. He promised them four shillings for each tree that had to be destroyed, plus two shillings each year for the next three years on each new tree they planted—considerably more than they had been reimbursed before—and assured them that the local agriculture field officers would help them protect their healthy trees. Such was his popularity that most farmers voluntarily co-operated.

Governor Arden-Clarke was pleased with the results of the speech, but Nkrumah did not escape some acrid comments from his opponents. His earlier support of the cocoa farmers against the government was summed up as political opportunism. Now that he had changed his mind, he was called a stooge of the British. Nkrumah felt that he could afford to dismiss his critics, justified or not. They were too few to bother about, or so it seemed.

A special meeting of the Legislative Assembly was called on March 5, 1952. The assembly meetings had become colorful affairs, and this was no exception. The chiefs were clad in ceremonial dress. The CPP assemblymen wore long robes draped over one shoulder, in the Akan tradition. Nkrumah favored the short tunic worn in the Northern Territories. Sir Emmanuel Quist, the Speaker, wore a long black gown and white curled wig, like a British magistrate. Business suits were predominant among the Opposition.

Governor Arden-Clarke addressed the assemblymen. Her Majesty's Government, he told them, felt that the title of Kwame Nkrumah, "Leader of Government Business," should be replaced by "Prime Minister." Henceforth the Prime Minister would rank ahead of the three ex-officio, or European, ministers in the Cabinet and next in precedence to the governor himself.

As soon as Nkrumah could escape the congratulations of his colleagues, he went home and demanded of his mother, "What does it feel like to be the mother of the first African Prime Minister?" She made no comment; only her eyes revealed her pride in him.

Nkrumah's new appointment still had to be approved by the assembly, which was done on March 21, by a vote of 45 to 31. When the results were made known, the CPP assemblymen burst out singing, "There is victory for us!" They continued until Sir Emmanuel Quist sternly demanded order.

The disgruntled Opposition dismissed the change in title as "a mere shadow that was being dangled before our eyes." Their gloom did not detract from the general delight. The next afternoon, as Nkrumah rode between Kojo Botsio and Komla Gbedemah in an open car, thousands walked in a procession before and after them. From the roof tops, markets and cafés, shouts of "Freedom!" filled the air. Some of the less informed thought that since Nkrumah was now Prime Minister, the Gold Coast was at last independent. He had to convince them that their struggle was far from over.

8

TACTICAL ACTION

God is busy growing cocoa.
—Gold Coast saying

After Nkrumah became Prime Minister, the CPP authorized
a motorcycle escort for him. Dressed in scarlet, the motor-
cyclists rode ahead, behind, and on both sides of his official
car, whenever he was driven through the streets of Accra or
into the countryside. His critics disapproved of this osten-
tation, but the people were delighted with it. "Kwame!"
they called to him when he passed, as he had encouraged
them to do. His associates and his secretary, a young Eng-
lishwoman named Erica Powell, now addressed him as
"P.M.," in the British manner.

Once in his new position Nkrumah replaced "Positive Action" with "Tactical Action." In effect this meant using stra-
tegic tactics—and tact—to get British consent and co-operation for Nkrumah's Five-Year Plan with its accompanying
social reforms. His old UGCC colleagues sneered that Tactical Action was "eating cake with the imperialists," and accused him of being ready to make deals with the same
profiteers who had exploited the Gold Coast in the past.

The Opposition attitude surfaced in connection with the
Volta River hydroelectric project. This was a mammoth un-
dertaking, originally conceived by Sir Gordon Guggisberg,
to harness the Volta River for electricity. On February 23,

1953, Nkrumah presented to the Legislative Assembly a motion to proceed on the negotiations for the project.

The scheme involved construction of a giant dam, which in turn would produce a huge man-made lake. It also called for the building of a new harbor at Tema, larger and more modern than the one at Takoradi, and of new railroads, factories, and housing. That would be just the beginning. The cost would be enormous but so were the potential benefits.

Electricity from the hydroelectric plant would be used to process bauxite into aluminum, providing the Gold Coast with an important new industry. Electricity would also be furnished to light Gold Coast homes cheaply and would be available to neighboring countries as well. The lake itself, stocked with fish, would provide a new and needed food supply.

Gold Coast reserves, now held in England, would supply part of the funds, but foreign capital would also be necessary.

It was on this point that a bitter debate took place on the assembly floor. Dr. Danquah charged that the Volta River plan paved the way for control "by the capitalists and imperialists." The scholarly Dr. Kofi Busia warned that "the sociological implications of the scheme" should have a second look and predicted that the project would mortgage their entire economic future. William Ofori Atta said sarcastically that the British had now become "imperialist angels."

Nkrumah finally lost his temper. "Do you think I am a fool to enter into a project like that blind?" he burst out angrily, adding that he had always been "one of the principal soldiers against imperialism."

No one could escape the irony that people who once had considered him too radical were now attacking him for not being radical enough. But because of Tactical Action he had British support on his motion, with the result that about half the chiefs voted with him. The final vote was fifty-one for and fourteen against. Nkrumah had won, and the Volta River project could get under way.

Through Tactical Action, Nkrumah's government also made a number of reforms, not as many as he wished but enough to be noticeable.

Under colonialism, the three provinces—the Colony, Ashanti, and the Northern Territories—were assigned to three chief commissioners, appointed by the governor. These men ruled their provinces like small kingdoms and lived in huge mansions surrounded by wide lawns and landscaped gardens. Contingents of soldiers and police guarded them.

The provinces were further divided up into areas supervised by district commissioners, also appointed by the governor, who lived almost as grandly. They had control of everything in their areas, even to dispensing justice and performing marriage ceremonies.

Nkrumah could not change this autocratic system, but with Governor Arden-Clarke's consent, the chief commissioners were renamed regional officers and the district commissioners became government agents. Nkrumah made it clear to them that they were no longer a law unto themselves, but were responsible to the central government. His interference with what they considered their just prerogatives was resented bitterly.

To give the people a share in local rule, Nkrumah set up local councils. Chiefs could serve on the councils but had no right to vote, while the former commissioners were excluded. In the first local government council elections in 1952, CPP candidates received 90 per cent of the seats in 270 new councils.

Other problems, besides the swollen shoot disease, faced the cocoa farmers. At least partially because of obligations to family and relatives, indebtedness was chronic with them. Nkrumah found out that the Colonial Agricultural Loans Board, set up to help them, had made only one loan to one farmer in its dozen years of existence. The CPP ministers disbanded the board in 1953 and set up the Cocoa Purchasing Company instead. In its first year of operation, the company loaned cocoa farmers over a million pounds.

The income of the cocoa farmers was always uncertain because the price of cocoa on the world market fluctuated so widely. In 1954, the Nkrumah government passed a bill giving farmers a fixed rate, no matter what the world price, with the proviso that any funds above that rate would be used to expand the economy. That year, the world price reached a record high of 562.10 pounds a ton, far above the fixed rate.

A group of Ashanti farmers, mostly the wealthier ones, seeing themselves deprived of substantial profits, organized the "Council for Higher Cocoa Prices." Their claim was that the funds which should have gone to Ashanti, were being diverted elsewhere in the country. Nkrumah appealed to their patriotism, pointing out the new library and new hospital being built in their capital of Kumasi, and the new highways which would benefit everyone, but they were not appeased. They and the Ashanti chiefs who supported them remained a source of discontent for as long as Nkrumah was in power.

On July 10, 1953, Nkrumah delivered his "Motion of Destiny" speech to the assembly. The motion called on the assembly to introduce an Act of Independence to the British Parliament, a necessary formality in applying constitutionally for self-government.

In this speech Nkrumah proposed that upon independence the Gold Coast should take the name of Ghana. The suggestion had originally come from Dr. Danquah, who from his research into African history had concluded that the ancestors of the Akan people had migrated from the ancient Kingdom of Ghana. Other scholars disputed his claim, showing evidence that the Akan came from other regions of the Sudan. The symbolic value of the name Ghana was undisputed. It seemed fitting to name the Gold Coast after the ancient African kingdom which had risen to such a high degree of civilization without European influence.

The second part of the Motion of Destiny called for the Legislative Assembly to be enlarged to 104 members, all elected directly by the people. This eliminated the power of the Provincial Councils of Chiefs to choose their own members. The passage of the motion made a new election necessary, and it was scheduled for June 15. Again Nkrumah toured the country, speaking in every rural village and hamlet.

All CPP branches of the 104 constituencies were requested to submit the names of their candidates to the CPP central committee in Accra for approval. In some cases the central committee arbitrarily passed over locally popular persons for others considered to have better leadership ability or greater loyalty to the party. Certain candidates, whose names were crossed out by the central committee, ran for office anyway. Nkrumah saw this as an attempt to split the ranks of the CPP, and the renegade candidates were expelled. The matter did not end there. A few of them ran as Independent candidates or joined the newly formed Northern People's Party, which had strength in the Northern Territories.

The party campaign slogan was "CPP 104," to show they intended to win all the seats. This was overly optimistic, but they did win 72, a sizable majority. The Northern People's Party won 12 of the 21 Northern Territories seats. The UGCC won nowhere. The sociology professor, Dr. Kofi Busia, received one seat for his Ghana Congress Party. He continued to be an admirer of what he called "the democratic institutions of Britain," and liked Nkrumah no better than before. A few scattered seats went to the Togoland Party, the Anlo Youth Organization, and the Moslem Association Party.

According to British parliamentary custom, the Northern People's Party, next largest to the CPP, became the Opposition party. Nkrumah objected that they represented only one region, but was overruled by Sir Emmanuel Quist, the Speaker. The charge was made against Nkrumah that he wanted a one-party state. He firmly denied it.

After the election, the rich cocoa farmers who had formed the Council for Higher Cocoa Prices, changed their name to the more patriotic-sounding National Liberation Movement. The Asantehene, Prempeh II, supported them. The main plank in the NLM platform was a demand for a federal government in which each territory would have greater autonomy. Nkrumah argued that this system would not work in a country as small as Ghana, where each province was dependent on the others; though Ashanti had most of the cocoa farms and the richest gold fields, they needed the labor of the Northern Territories and the shipping facilities of the Colony.

The NLM remained opposed to him. In the next weeks violence broke out in Ashanti against the local CPP members. Hundreds of them fled to other regions. The sister of Krobo Edusei, CPP national propaganda secretary, was shot down and killed and his wife's house was burned. Several chiefs sympathetic to the CPP were de-stooled.

The British press put the blame for the trouble on Nkrumah. Actually he had ordered his CPP people in Ashanti not to retaliate. His great fear was that civil war might break out and make the British think twice about granting independence. At all costs he felt a peaceful solution must be sought.

In the manner of an Akan chief summoning the village elders to a council meeting, he invited the NLM leaders to a round-table conference to discuss their differences. They refused to come. In the assembly, Nkrumah moved that a select committee be appointed "to examine the question of a federal system of government for the Gold Coast." Dr. Busia, who had taken a stand with the NLM, walked out with twenty Opposition members. The select committee was appointed without them. After holding a long series of meetings and studying many documents, they reported their decision not to recommend a federal form of government.

The violence spread from Ashanti to other areas. On November 10, 1955, at about eight in the evening, Nkrumah was sitting on an upstairs verandah of his house with several colleagues, when two explosions came in rapid succession and a bright orange glow lit up the back of the house. All the windows were shattered, but no one was hurt.

The police reported that enough gelignite had been used to destroy the house and everyone in it, but that it had been badly placed. They never found the culprits. Nkrumah was probably correct in feeling that the NLM and the Opposition had a hand in the attempted assassination.

The official British position had been to keep aloof from the Ashanti struggle, but in March 1956, the Secretary of State for the Colonies, A. T. Lennox-Boyd, let it be known that because of the dissension, it was felt that another election should be held before the country was launched on independence. Her Majesty's Government wanted to make sure, he said, that a reasonable majority really wanted independence in the near future and could agree on a workable constitution.

No such demand was made of other British colonies, not even in South Africa where nonwhites were not allowed to vote. Nkrumah was probably as near total discouragement as he ever allowed himself to be. Everyone had been hoping for independence in 1956. That was now impossible. Nkrumah did not want another election now, fearing it would mean more violence. He yielded since the only other choice was to defy the British and declare independence anyway.

The election was scheduled for July. In the campaign, Nkrumah stuck to the one main issue: a federal form of government demanded by the NLM and their allies, versus a unitary government. There was no violence. The CPP won 71 seats, increased later to 72 by one of the Independents. It was far more than the "reasonable majority" the Secretary of State had demanded. The sterile debate about federalism was at last a dead issue. Nkrumah could forget it and look back at some of the real achievements of his government.

Eighteen new agricultural stations had been set up and four new agricultural training centers built. Many miles of new railroads and highways had been constructed. The capacity of Takoradi Harbor had been increased. The new harbor at Tema was under way. Several major bridges had been completed and others started. There were thirteen new post office buildings. Some five thousand new telephones had been installed.

The housing program had provided 15,000 units, housing 45,000 persons. Rural electricity was increasing. Nearly a thousand wells had been sunk and many water pipes installed. Nine new hospitals were completed or under construction and existing hospitals were being expanded. Two new health centers were ready.

The government-sponsored Ambassador Hotel in Accra had a hundred bedrooms with private baths, lounges, bars, a restaurant, and a banquet hall that would seat three hundred persons. The hotel would give tourists and other visitors the finest accommodations they could find anywhere.

Other imposing official buildings were springing up in Accra, designed by the British architect Maxwell Fry. One of them was the African Community Center, a large, airy structure with a bas-relief over the entrance showing Ashanti chiefs beneath their large umbrellas.

View of Elmina Castle, built by the Portuguese in 1481, near modern Cape Coast. *(United Nations)*

Family life in the old Gold Coast. The man of the house dines alone and in style, albeit his table is made from a packing box from England. *(Pix, Inc.)*

American college student. *(Panaf Books, Ltd., 89 Fleet Street, London E.C.4, for photographs from* Ghana: Autobiography of Kwame Nkrumah, *First published in London in 1957.)*

Geoffrey Bing, Labour Member of Parliament, who became Nkrumah's close adviser and friend. *(Pix, Inc.)*

Dr. Joseph Boakye Danquah, founder and first president of the United Gold Coast Convention. *(Pix, Inc.)*

Krobo Edusei *(Pix, Inc.)*

Students at Aggrey House, Achimota College, in 1929. Nkrumah is seated, first on the left. *(Panaf Books, Ltd., 89 Fleet St., London E.C.4, for photographs from* Ghana: Autobiography of Kwame Nkrumah, *First published in London in 1957.)*

Nkrumah (right) with his mother and his friend, Ackah Watson, at Tarkwa shortly after his return to the Gold Coast from England. *(Panaf Books, Ltd., 89 Fleet St., London E.C.4, for photographs from* Ghana: Autobiography of Kwame Nkrumah, *First published in London in 1957.)*

Komla Gbedemah *(Pix, Inc.)*

From prison, Nkrumah gave directives for his Convention People's Party in the Gold Coast's first general election, February 1951. This note, addressed to Gbedemah, was written on a sheet of toilet paper with a stub of a pencil. *(Panaf Books, Ltd., 89 Fleet St., London E.C.4, for photographs from* Ghana: Autobiography of Kwame Nkrumah, *First published in London in 1957.)*

IMPortant

Dear Kob.

I have read the draft of the Manifesto. It is a good work done and much labour has been expended on it. You and Lamptey deserve my congratulation for such comprehensive document.

However, it is too elaborate to serve as a Manifesto for an election campaign; that of an election campaign should be short, brief, simple direct, popular and

A mammoth crowd greeted Nkrumah when he was released from prison following the CPP landslide victory in the general election. (*Panaf Books, Ltd., 89 Fleet St., London E.C.4, for photographs from* Ghana: Autobiography of Kwame Nkrumah, *First published in London in 1957.)*

Two Gold Coast farmers searching for signs of the dread swollen shoot disease in their cocoa plantation. As Leader of Government Business, Nkrumah had the unpleasant task of persuading cocoa farmers to destroy all trees showing signs of this disease. (*Pix, Inc.)*

Prior to Independence, Nkrumah co-operated with Sir Charles Arden-Clarke, Gold Coast governor, first as Leader of Government Business, then as Prime Minister. *(Pix, Inc.)*

At Lincoln University, Pennsylvania, June 5, 1951, with President Horace M. Bond, who presented Nkrumah with the honorary degree of doctor of laws. Left rear is Kojo Botsio, who accompanied Nkrumah to America. *(Panaf Books, Ltd., 89 Fleet St., London E.C.4, for photographs from* Ghana: Autobiography of Kwame Nkrumah, *First published in London in 1957.)*

As President of Ghana, Nkrumah addresses the UN General Assembly September 1960. He wears the traditional Ghana robe of kente cloth. *(United Nations)*

It has become fashionable in the new African nations for citizens to wear garments of cloth emblazoned with the portraits of their leaders. *(Pix, Inc.)*

A thrilling moment in the history of Nkrumah's Ghana—when the two gates of a diversion tunnel of the Volta Dam close and thus start the formation of the great Volta Lake. *(Pix, Inc.)*

In the 1954 Gold Coast elections, conscientious campaigners with police guard (in cap) paddle ballot boxes across a river in Ashanti territory to the nearest counting station. *(Keystone)*

Prime Minister Nkrumah is carried shoulder-high by his supporters after the victory of his Convention People's Party in the 1954 elections. *(Pix, Inc.)*

Nkrumah's all-African Cabinet, 1954–56. Seated, left to right: Archie Casely-Hayford, Kojo Botsio, Nkrumah, Komla Gbedemah, E. O. Asafu-Adjaye. Standing, left to right: J. H. Allassani, N. A. Welbeck, A. E. Ofori-Atta, Ako Adjei, J. E. Jantuah, Imoru Egala. *(Authenticated News Service)*

After Independence, this twenty-foot statue of "Kwame Nkrumah Founder of the Nation" was erected in front of Parliament House. *(United Nations)*

Festivities and dancing in Tamale in the Northern Territories in honor of President Nkrumah. *(Marc Ribaud, Magnum)*

Nkrumah with his beautiful Egyptian wife, Fathia Helen Ritzk, and their first two children, Gorke Gamal and Samia Yabah. *(United Press International)*

President Nkrumah addressing the first session of the second parliament of Republic of Ghana. *(Pix, Inc.)*

Under Nkrumah's leadership of the Gold Coast modern buildings sprang up in Accra, some, like these, in green fields where goats still grazed. *Magnum)*

Under Nkrumah, Tema became Ghana's first modern harbor. In Gold Coast days, ships anchored far out at Takoradi; Cargo had to be unloaded at sea and rowed to shore. *(Marc Ribaud, Magnum)*

A Ghanaian soldier, in the red tunic and blue trousers of the Guards, faints from the oppressive heat, in Black Star Square, Accra. The new nation did not free itself overnight from certain unsuitable British customs, such as heavy woolen uniforms for police and soldiers. *(Pix, Inc.)*

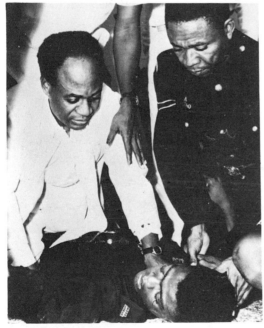

President Nkrumah leans thoughtfully over Constable Seth Ametewee, who has just fired five shots at him in an unsuccessful assassination attempt. One of the shots killed police superintendent Salifu Dagarti, for which murder Seth Ametewee was later condemned to hang—the nearest to a political execution during Nkrumah's entire rule. *(Pix, Inc.)*

Dr. Conor Cruise O'Brien, former UN delegate from Ireland, who was briefly vice-chancellor of the University of Ghana. *(Pix, Inc.)*

John W. K. Harlley, whom Nkrumah appointed as Commissioner of Police, after Seth Ametewee's assassination attempt, became a leader of the military coup which overthrew Nkrumah. *(Africa Report)*

Major (later Brigadier General) Akwasi Afrifa. *(Africa Report)*

Colonel (later Major General) E. K. Kotoka. *(Pix, Inc.)*

Major General J. A. Ankrah. *(Africa Report)*

Dr. Kofi Busia, former sociology professor and long Nkrumah's political opponent, became Prime Minister of Ghana in September 1969, a post he held until a second military coup in January 1972. *(Africa Report)*

Nkrumah in exile, with President Sékou Touré (sixth from right) and other Guinean friends. *(Authenticated News International)*

Nkrumah's twenty-foot statue was not demolished and beheaded by "jubilant Ghanaians," as reported in the Western press, but by a demolition crew sent in by Ghana's new rulers the day after their coup. *(Pix, Inc.)*

After Nkrumah's forced departure, many of his projects were neglected. Typical is this irrigation canal at Asutsuare, choked with weeds. To restore it, the UN Development Program in 1968 sponsored a pilot irrigation scheme to produce rice. *(United Nations)*

Regular educational broadcasts were being given in English and several African languages. One program gave summaries of the Legislative Assembly proceedings, scrupulously including the speeches of the Opposition.

There had been great progress in education, the project dearest to Nkrumah. Primary schools had more than doubled, and there were twice as many students in secondary schools. Eight new teacher-training colleges had been opened. The College of Technology at Kumasi and University College of Ghana at Legon, both started by the British, were now completed. But Nkrumah's dream of wiping out illiteracy and providing free and compulsory education for all was still far from fulfilled. Nor had he yet been able to launch the national health service he wanted, for lack of doctors, nurses, and medical staff.

There had been a couple of scandals. J. A. Braimah, one of Nkrumah's non-CPP ministers, had confessed to taking 2,000 pounds as a gift from a contractor engaged to build a training college in the Northern Territories. The Cocoa Purchasing Company was also being accused of taking gifts from farmers in return for loans. A Commission of Inquiry, appointed by Nkrumah, was still trying to get the facts.

On the whole, what had been accomplished was phenomenal. It was already said of Nkrumah that whatever he wanted done had to be done yesterday.

On September 17, 1956, Governor Arden-Clarke requested Nkrumah's presence at Christiansborg. The ancient castle was now familiar territory to him. In the huge cabinet room, lined with portraits of former British governors, he and his cabinet ministers had threshed out their problems with Sir Charles, week after week. Romantic-looking on the outside, the castle's rooms and apartments were dank and damp because of the ocean spray cascading on its sea walls. Still it was a historic place, and when Nkrumah saw the grin

with which the governor greeted him, he guessed that this
was a historic occasion.

Sir Charles handed him a dispatch from the Secretary of
State. The fifth paragraph contained the long-awaited message: "Her Majesty's Government intends that full Independence could come about on the 6th March, 1957." Her
Majesty's Government would take the legal steps needed to
give the country the name of Ghana.

The document included a clause about Trans Volta/Togo.
Some of this territory's Ewe population had expressed a desire to be united with the Ewes in French Togoland, but a
plebiscite sponsored by the United Nations had resulted in
a 58 per cent vote for union with the Gold Coast. Now the
Secretary of State decreed that the "Trust Territory of Togoland" would be included within the independent Gold
Coast. That, too, was good news for Nkrumah, who had not
wanted the split.

The next morning he told the assembly that independence had been granted. A second of silence was followed
by pandemonium. Some members cheered, others wept.
Even the Opposition was moved.

While the whole country was rejoicing, Nkrumah and his
cabinet held lengthy conferences with their British colleagues about Ghana's new constitution. With them was
Geoffrey Bing, the Labour Member of Parliament Nkrumah
had met in London, who had now joined his government as
constitutional adviser. Never had an outside adviser been
more needed.

Great Britain had assumed the right to prepare the constitution. Their version was complicated by their insistence
on including safeguards for the 519 pensionable British Colonial civil servants who would be working with independent Ghana. By the liberal compensation terms the British
demanded, any official with ten years' service in any colony,
if he was stationed in Ghana in 1954 and was forty-one or

forty-two years old, could retire with a bonus of 8,000 pounds. (Younger men would draw proportionately less.) Although the total sum ran into millions, Nkrumah and his cabinet had not objected. Krobo Edusei commented that it was natural the British should require a "gift"—that is, a bribe—before they left.

What did bother Nkrumah was that the clauses and sub-clauses about the pensions and compensations, which included constant references to past constitutions, made the new constitution almost unreadable. He had wanted a constitution written in simple language that anyone could understand. At his request, Geoffrey Bing prepared a sample draft, which after the cabinet ministers had discussed it and corrected it was sent to London. The Secretary of State of the Colonial Office promptly rejected it. Things had to be done the British way until independence was a reality.

The British also planned the independence ceremonies. Nkrumah was first told that the ceremonies would be based on those of Ceylon, to whom England had granted independence under the Commonwealth in 1948. About a month before Ghana's independence, the Colonial Office decreed that the ceremonies were to be based on the precedent set for Australia's independence.

Australia had become an independent British Commonwealth nation in 1901. No one seemed to know what had been done. Cables were sent to various Australian officials. Someone finally remembered that on the great day, Australian Members of Parliament had assembled at the Science Museum and, accompanied by a mass choir, had sung "Rule Britannia." It hardly seemed appropriate for Ghana.

Nkrumah sent a mission to London to find out exactly what the Colonial Office had in mind by the "Australian precedent." The Colonial Office referred the mission to Buckingham Palace, who in turn referred it to the Lord Chancellor, who knew nothing. At the last moment, the Colonial Office gave notice that Ghana was to return to the Ceylon precedent.

Geoffrey Bing was impressed by Nkrumah's calm and patience through all this rigmarole. He was, Bing wrote later, "much more civilized in a curiously sophisticated way than the British politicians and Colonial civil servants with whom he was contending." For Nkrumah, only one thing was important. The last obstacle had been hurdled. Tactical Action had achieved its primary aim.

9

A COMMONWEALTH NATION

We shall measure our progress by the improvement in
the health of our people; by the number of children in
school, and by the availability of water and electricity
in our towns and villages, and by the happiness which
our people take in being able to manage their own affairs.

—NKRUMAH

From all over the country, men, women, and children
streamed into Accra, mostly on foot, to witness the Independence Day ceremonies. Scores of aircraft brought delegations from fifty-eight nations, along with foreign journalists
and photographers. Vice-President Richard Nixon represented the United States. Queen Elizabeth sent her aunt, the
Duchess of Kent, to represent Great Britain. Eighteen African territories sent representatives. Even the Union of
South Africa, where no nonwhite man or woman could vote,
sent a representative.

A triumphal arch was erected near the site where the ex-
servicemen's march had been fired upon by the police in
1948. The veterans were now recognized as Ghana's first
martyrs for freedom. There were fireworks every night.
There were races of fishing canoes. There was a religious
ceremony in which the Chief of the Ga people poured a
libation as an offering to ancient gods. On March 4, 1957, a
state banquet was held at the splendid new Ambassador
Hotel in honor of the foreign diplomats.

"In two days time our colonial relationship with Britain will end," said Nkrumah in his welcoming speech, "but we part with the warmest feelings of goodwill . . . We hope this will be the beginning of a much closer association." His speech set the mood of the occasion. The transfer of power resembled more a parting of friends than a severance of ties between a colonial people and their European masters.

On the eve of Independence, Nkrumah addressed the Legislative Assembly for the last time as Prime Minister of the Gold Coast colony. He took stock of their country's material resources in minerals and cocoa and said that Ghana's annual wealth averaged just over fifty pounds for each person, small compared to Great Britain but far higher than most African and Asian countries. He felt that they would be able to stand on their own feet.

His speech ended with a note of warning about the effect of their independence on other African territories: their success or failure to make Ghana "into a prosperous and happy state" would have consequences far beyond their own frontiers. Their failure would have tragic effects for all of Africa. "We must not fail! We shall not fail!"

Later Nkrumah drove to the Polo Grounds, where a hundred thousand people or more were waiting expectantly. At the stroke of midnight, the Union Jack was lowered, and the flag of Ghana—red, white, and green horizontal stripes, with a five-pointed black star centered on the white strip—was raised. Bands played Ghana's national anthem, "Lift High the Flag of Ghana," amidst joyous cries of "Freedom!"

A few weeks after Independence Day, Nkrumah's Cabinet voted to erect a twenty-foot statue of him, wearing his Northern Territories tunic and with his hand raised in the Freedom salute, in front of the Parliament building. At the same time the Cabinet decided to issue a new currency, on which the head of Nkrumah would be shown. There was a great deal of caustic comment about the new coinage from people who would not have dreamed of criticizing Queen Elizabeth for letting her likeness appear on British coinage. In a television interview Nkrumah commented that the coinage was a way of impressing his people that Ghana really was independent.

During all the long years of the struggle for independence, Nkrumah had remained a bachelor. In December 1957, to the surprise of almost everyone, the newspapers announced his marriage. His bride was a beautiful dark-haired Egyptian, Fathia Helen Ritzk. The marriage ceremony had been small and private. Only Nkrumah's mother, the bride's uncle, and a few of Nkrumah's very close friends were present.

Nkrumah took his bride to Christiansborg Castle, now renamed Osu Castle. They occupied a small apartment on half the top story. The living room opened onto a balcony overlooking the sea. Another larger balcony, looking over the courtyard, was used as a second living room. There was one large bedroom with bath, two guest bedrooms with a shared bathroom, and a small room which Madame Nkrumah converted into a kitchen.

Most of the rest of the huge castle, once the governor's residence, was transformed into office space. The large salons were used only for official receptions. A great deal of fanfare attended Nkrumah's public appearances, but he preferred simplicity in his private life. Friends dropped in at the castle informally. He liked to sit with them on the balcony and watch the tropical sunsets over the sea. He would take a drink to keep them company but usually left it unfinished. At dinners, British protocol was ignored. His steward served wives of minor civil servants before the Prime Minister.

For a number of years Nkrumah's favorite hobby had been growing roses. He enjoyed good motion pictures and classical music. He always found time to read and acquired an excellent library of books on Africa, some of them rare and long out of print.

Madame Nkrumah rarely appeared with him at public functions, nor did she accompany him on his foreign tours. The wife of Geoffrey Bing, now Nkrumah's Attorney General, gave her English lessons. Sometimes the four of them went on picnics to the beach in the Bings' car, with Mrs. Bing driving and no security guards in sight. A year after Nkrumah's marriage, his first son was born, Gorke Gamal Nkrumah. He was named "Gamal" after President Nasser of Egypt, one of Nkrumah's good friends. A girl was born two years later, Samia Yabah Nkrumah. A third child was another boy, Seku Ritzk Nkrumah.

A few months after Independence, the National Liberation Movement in Ashanti and their allies formed the United Party. They drew into their ranks the former Northern People's Party and those of the Ewe people in Togoland who had voted against union with Ghana. Dr. Kofi Busia and the former UGCC leaders, Dr. Danquah and Obetsebi Lamptey, were active in the United Party, which became the official Opposition. As time went on it became clear to Nkrumah that they were not going to limit themselves to vocal opposition, but were engaging in conspiracies to stir up trouble with the aim of destroying him and his government.

In essence the United Party was a union of intellectuals and frustrated chiefs, still indignant at the loss of Indirect Rule. Nkrumah did not minimize the danger, but he could not expect the outside world, now watching Ghana so closely, to believe that these prosperous Oxford and Cambridge graduates, and the picturesque African chiefs with their umbrellas and ceremonial rites, were a real threat to Ghana's future.

In August, the Ghana parliament had enacted a Deportation Act, not a new act but a consolidation of two British colonial laws. About a sixth of Ghana's near six million population were aliens, mostly from other parts of Africa. The colonial government had always deported the undesirables.

When a Nigerian in Kumasi took the title of "Zeriken Zongo"
—chief of the non-Ghanaian Moslems—and fighting broke
out among his followers, the British had deported him immediately.

Early in 1958, another Nigerian proclaimed himself the
new Zeriken Zongo. Still another called himself the Chaplain
of the Hausa people in Kumasi. The Hausa, most of whom
came from Northern Nigeria, had a reputation for being easily incited to tribal warfare, and there were constant disturbances around the "chaplain's" mosque. The Nkrumah
government took both Nigerians into custody and transferred
them to Accra. While they were awaiting trial, their supporters attacked several police and wounded a European
government official. In an attempt to avoid further trouble,
the two Nigerians were deported.

The third person deported under the Act was a Dr. Emil
Savundra, well recommended by London, who claimed to be
a financier, an investor, and a Christian deeply opposed to
colonialism. At first glance his proposal to set up a con-
sortium to take over mineral rights and help the gold mining
companies out of financial difficulties seemed favorable to
the government. But some of his actions aroused suspicion,
and inspectors were sent to check his books. It turned out
that Savundra kept no books, but the inspectors did find a
copy of a letter from him to a Member of British Parliament,
saying that it was easy to fool the Africans. He, too, was deported.

The deportation of the two Nigerians and Dr. Savundra
brought protests in the British press. The reactionary *Daily
Telegraph* was especially vicious. The three men were "the
first batch of foreign investors to be deported." Nkrumah was
governing Ghana in an "arbitrary and oppressive way."
Ghana had become "a corrupt, cruel and vulgar tyranny."
The *Telegraph* was particularly abusive toward British civil
servants who had refused the 8,000-pound compensation

and were staying on in the new government. Nkrumah had no right to expect British assistance; he should "do his own dirty work."

From the rabid tone of the articles, Nkrumah deduced that already "imperialists" were trying to undermine Ghana's independence, perhaps with the complicity of the Opposition.

In December 1957, Krobo Edusei, Minister of the Interior, had suggested a Preventive Detention Act, modeled on one already in force in India. Nkrumah and the other cabinet members rejected the proposal. Detention without trial was not something they wanted in Ghana, regardless of how often it was used elsewhere. A subsequent series of events caused them to reconsider.

A secret organization sprang up in Accra called the Ga Shifimo Kpee, made up of Ga people with strong tribal feelings who resented the non-Ga people moving into Accra. Their meetings were held secretly in darkened rooms with the speakers masked. Police reported that several of their leaders had criminal records. A parliament member named Modesto Apaloo, Deputy Leader of the Opposition, was said to have addressed one of their meetings. The Avoidance of Discrimination Act made the organization of religious, tribal or regional parties illegal, but there was not enough known about the Ga Shifimo Kpee to bring any of the leaders to trial.

In the same period a rather odd police report came in. It seemed that another Opposition parliament member, R. R. Amponsah, General Secretary of the United Party, had purchased in London enough badges of rank to convert fifty non-commissioned officers to lieutenants and captains. There was nothing illegal about such a purchase, but no one could deny that it was suspicious.

It was in view of the Hausa violence, the Ga conspiracy,

and the Amponsah matter, that a modified version of the India Preventive Detention Act was passed. Many parliament members deplored the measure. Nkrumah disliked it but viewed it as a necessary precaution. The act provided for detention up to five years. The detainee had to be served with written details of the grounds of his detention. He was given an opportunity to appeal to the Cabinet against them, or could bring his case before the courts by *habeas corpus* proceedings.

On December 1958, two days before Nkrumah was scheduled to go to India, a certain Lieutenant Amenyah went to a senior British officer and reported that the Camp Commander of the Accra Garrison, Major Benjamin Awhaitey, had been approached by the two members of parliament, R. R. Amponsah and Modesto Apaloo, who brought with them some army uniforms and badges of rank, along with fifty pounds cash. The members of parliament wanted Awhaitey to use the money to bribe some non-commissioned officers to assassinate Nkrumah as he boarded the aircraft for India. Awhaitey had later called in Lieutenant Amenyah and asked him to meet Amponsah and Apaloo at the meeting place they had set and to tell them that Awhaitey could not arrange the assassination.

Army authorities promptly arrested Major Awhaitey on the charge of failing to report what he knew of a proposed coup d'état. At his military court-martial, he gave more than four versions of the same incidents, but he did admit that Amponsah had asked his help to overthrow the government. It was obvious that he knew more than he would say. His penalty was dismissal from service.

In the meantime three senior officers went to the place where Major Awhaitey had told Lieutenant Amenyah to meet the two members of parliament. They found Amponsah alone in his car. When they asked him what he was doing, he said he was waiting for Modesto Apaloo. They arrested him and later Apaloo. Both were held under the Preventive Detention Act, the first time it had been used.

The passage of the Preventive Detention Act, followed so closely by the detention of two members of parliament, shocked Nkrumah's closest friends and gave the Western press an easy target. Nkrumah's opponents called the act "intolerable in the Western world and repugnant to British justice."

This was somewhat hypocritical, since there had been no criticism when the much stronger preventive detention act was established in India. Nkrumah and the rest of the UGCC "Big Six" had been detained without trial for eight weeks in 1948 with no adverse comments from the press. At one time the British colonial government of Kenya held 38,000 Africans in preventive detention in Kenya. Eleven of them were beaten to death by their prison guards. Detention of non-whites and their sympathizers was even then common in South Africa.

Both Amponsah and Apaloo insisted that the story of a plot was fabricated by the Nkrumah government. Nkrumah determined that they should have a fair hearing and that the whole world would be witness to it. Dr. Kofi Busia, who might have been helpful, left Ghana to avoid testifying and did not return as long as Nkrumah was in power.

A tribunal was set up to investigate the matter, headed by a distinguished English barrister, Gilbert Granville Sharp; the conservative Ghanaian barrister Sir Tsibu Darku; and a West Indian senior magistrate, Maurice Charles. All three were notably impartial. A team of stenographers was flown in from English courts. Evidence from ninety-seven witnesses was taken in six languages.

A London merchant, brought to Accra, testified that Amponsah had spent 130 pounds on badges worn by army captains and lieutenants, officer swagger canes, and Sam Browne belts. It was discovered that Amponsah had ordered from another shop fifty officers' "hackles"—plumes worn in tropical headgear by Ghanaian officers—that he had them sent to Lomé, in Togo, and that Apaloo had collected them through an intermediary. Neither Amponsah nor Apaloo gave any convincing reasons for these purchases. The Special Branch of the security police reported a conversation overheard in a foreign embassy between Dr. Danquah and a diplomat unfriendly to Ghana. Danquah had assured the diplomat that everything was planned and that the Army would overthrow Nkrumah by Christmas.

The tribunal rejected some testimony against the two men on the grounds that it might have been inspired by jealousy. Throughout the proceedings they labored under considerable difficulty. In England, detection of crime depends largely on the testimony of literate policemen, whereas in Ghana less than a quarter of the police were literate. Records were few in Ghana; everything depended on personal recollections. Interpreters were unable to cope adequately with the variations in local dialects, which resulted in a certain amount of confusion.

In their final report the tribunal agreed unanimously that neither the police officers nor Nkrumah and his cabinet had concocted the case. All three judges found that Amponsah and Apaloo "since June 1958, were engaged in a conspiracy to carry out at some future date in Ghana, an act for unlawful purpose, revolutionary in character." In a majority report, Sir Tsibu Darku and Maurice Charles found that Awhaitey, Amponsah, and Apaloo "were engaged in a conspiracy to assassinate Nkrumah and carry out a coup d'état." Justice Granville Sharp in a minority report declared that Amponsah and Apaloo had withdrawn from the conspiracy when they suspected the police knew about it. What the three reports failed to do was to declare Amponsah and Apaloo either guilty or innocent of a specific crime.

To prove to his critics that every effort had been made to examine the case objectively, Nkrumah authorized a paperback edition of the tribunal proceedings. It weighed over four pounds. A copy was sent by airmail to every member of the International Commission of Jurists who had spoken unfavorably of Ghana's Preventive Detention Act. The only reply was from a Japanese jurist who congratulated the government printer on his choice of type. Copies were also sent to the Western press, along with an analysis, but even newspapers which had given the most space to Ghana affairs hardly mentioned the tribunal findings.

Up until this time Nkrumah had been deeply concerned about overseas opinion. It is said that this experience changed him. From now on, he decided, he would do whatever he felt was necessary to hold his government together, regardless of what the Western world said about it.

The vast majority of Ghanaians, Nkrumah's masses, were unaware that foreign newspapers had already condemned their leader and his government. What they knew and saw was that the magic word "freedom" was bringing numerous changes.

Ghana's first shipping line, the Black Star, was launched at Takoradi with an ocean-going merchant ship, the S.S. *Volta River*. The Bank of Ghana was opened in Accra, the country's first national banking institution. Ghana Airways was established with Ghanaian pilots, and this was followed by a Flying Training School, staffed by members of the Israel Air Force, and the recruitment of a Ghana Air Force.

Other experts from foreign countries, mostly British and American, came to give their services and advice to the new nation—agriculturists, architects, mining engineers, construction men. Doctors came to staff the new hospitals. Teachers and professors arrived to teach in the new primary and secondary schools.

Several thousand Ghana youths were sent abroad at government expense to study in foreign universities. For those who lacked university credits, jobs were opening up at home, in the new factories and industries, in the Builders Brigade, which worked on railroads or highways, or the Workers Brigade, which cleared land and planted crops on government state farms. Children could join the Young Pioneers, who, like the Boy Scouts, helped in community projects. The prospect of steady employment attracted Africans from less fortunate neighboring countries.

The people of Ghana were still poor and were working harder than ever, but there was a new pride about them. It was their country now, and they were building its future.

They took pleasure in their leader's frequent trips abroad, where he was received with all the honors of any world leader. There was a trip to England to meet with other British Commonwealth prime ministers. There was a flight to Canada to talk with Prime Minister Diefenbaker, and another trip to America, where President Eisenhower, "a cheerful, rosy-cheeked man" gave a luncheon in Nkrumah's honor at the White House. There was the trip to India, at the invitation of Prime Minister Nehru, which Nkrumah's enemies had allegedly planned to stop by his assassination. The University of New Delhi gave Nkrumah an honorary doctorate of letters, and he had a chance to thank the heads of this and other institutions for accepting and training Ghanaian students. A tiger shoot was arranged for him by the Maharaja of Mysore. No tigers showed up, but a rogue elephant charged the party, causing excitement enough.

On July 1, 1959, two weeks after the tenth anniversary of the Convention People's Party, Prime Minister Nkrumah announced the launching of the Second Five Year Development Plan. This included completing the Volta River Dam project and building six hundred new factories. The Western press, so fascinated by the troubles in Ashanti, the Ga tribal conspiracy, the Deportation Act, and the Preventive Detention

Act, took no notice of the Plan, except for a few snide comments.

Nearly a year later, the Ghana Government took a further step toward strengthening the nation's independence. In April 1960, a plebiscite was held to vote on a new constitution which would make Ghana a republic, but still within the British Commonwealth. Whereas up until now the Queen of England had remained Ghana's head of state, by the new constitution the country would elect a President, who combined the duties of both Prime Minister and head of state.

Nkrumah took the unusual step of inviting all African and Commonwealth countries to observe the election. In this way he hoped to avert any accusations of unfair voting practices. The Commonwealth countries did not accept. Prime Minister Nehru of India reproached Nkrumah for issuing the invitation, on the grounds that it would set a precedent for outside interference. Nkrumah had not foreseen this reaction and was hurt.

The United Party's presidential candidate was Dr. Joseph Danquah, who received 124,623 votes compared to 1,016,076 for Nkrumah. The Opposition claimed that they were unable to campaign properly. Moreover, there were allegations, apparently well founded, of falsification of voting returns, not in Accra but in outlying districts. So far as could be determined, police and civil servants in charge of the voting polls were responsible for the irregularities, either directly or by their acquiescence. There was no evidence that Nkrumah was involved and much to show that he wanted the elections to be fair. There were some accusations that the Opposition had purposely manipulated the false voting in order to bring the Nkrumah government into disrepute, knowing that they had no hope of winning the election.

The ceremonies of July 1, 1960, proclaiming Ghana a republic were on an even grander scale than those three years before at Independence Day. Dignitaries came from all over the world in greater numbers than before. Bells tolled and ships in the Accra harbor blew their sirens. People thronged the streets shouting "Long live Osagyefo [the Redeemer] Kwame Nkrumah!"

In the State House, before a gathering of Ghana's distinguished guests, the new President mounted the dais, flanked by senior Ghanaian army officers in ceremonial dress. Holding in his right hand the double-bladed solid gold Sword of State, the traditional symbol of peace, he took a solemn oath administered by Chief Justice, Sir Arku Korsah.

A new and crucial era in Ghana's history was launched.

10

PRESIDENT OF THE REPUBLIC

> The king knows each day what is happening in the
> most humble village in his empire; from all sides he
> receives reports and minute details.
>
> —Nineteenth-century visitor to Ashanti

In the spring of 1961, the British Guiana author of *To Sir,
With Love*, E. R. Braithwaite, visited Ghana, curious to see
what life was like in black Africa's first independent nation.
He found the lounge of the Accra airport hotel crowded with
people of many nationalities—Indians with their wives in
colorful saris, British army sergeants drinking beer, Lebanese
holding a birthday celebration, Germans, French, Americans,
Czechs, and African men and women in national dress.
Waiters supplied frosted drinks. A native peddler sat cross-
legged beside a display of African craft and handiwork.
Above the lounge chatter the roar of huge bulldozers and
tractor graders could be heard. Amid thick clouds of red
dust, work was in progress to enlarge the airport runway.

Near the airport a housing site of two-story homes spread
out over a grassy knoll. This was one of the new villages for
war veterans. Each family had a parcel of land beyond the
village for a garden. The smooth macadam road to Accra
went past English-style bungalows with trimmed hedges and
beneath roadway arches decorated with the red, white and
green stripes of the Ghana flag. There was an air of cleanli-
ness and order.

Central Accra was as modern as any European or American city. The new Trade Union Building and the Co-op Building were colorfully painted. There were green lawns and trees around them. The new cathedral was modern in design. The headquarters of the Convention People's Party was of pastel shades. The murals inside depicted Ghana's struggle for independence. There was still a slum section in Accra, with littered streets and shanty houses, but people assured Braithwaite that this remnant of the old days would disappear as new housing became available. At a night club, Europeans and Africans danced together.

In contrast to the market women in native dress and turbans, there were young businesswomen in trim suits, bareheaded, their hair stylishly dressed. In the new Ghana women were taking their place beside men in civil service, industry, and the professions. Waitresses in a fashionable restaurant wore attractive uniforms. Girls were eager to get this work, which was well-paid and dignified—no tipping was allowed. Under the British, only African men served as waiters and personal servants.

A smooth paved road led to Kumasi, once the stronghold of the Ashanti chiefs. Along the way were primitive African villages of thatched huts, but people seemed cheerful and well-fed, and their shops were well-stocked and neat. In one hamlet Braithwaite's party stopped to make a telephone call to Kumasi. Telephone service was no longer limited to the cities.

Kumasi seemed even newer than Accra, with bright homes, stores, motion-picture houses, blocks of apartment buildings. At night the visitors slept in a government bungalow, equipped with bath, electricity, and a refrigerator.

One of the showplaces of Kumasi was the Cultural Center, set in a pleasant park. It had been built to preserve the old and traditional and encourage new and experimental art. The main display was a full-sized reproduction of an Ashanti chieftain's house, as it was when the Ashanti were still fighting the British, built around a courtyard with a Tree of Truth in the center. Inside were exhibits of the ancient chiefs' fine-textured royal garments, beds, stools, talking drums. Close by, in a modern museum of stone and glass, was an exhibition of bronze and wood carvings done by a contemporary Kumasi doctor.

It was part of Nkrumah's long-range planning to bring culture and the benefits of modern technology to all Ghana's towns, so as to prevent heavy migration to the large centers, such as Accra. If all went on schedule, the impoverished Northern Territories, where generations of young men had flocked south in search of work, would be transformed into a prosperous industrial region.

The signs of progress Braithwaite saw marked the first stages of the Second Five Year Development Plan, through which Nkrumah obviously aimed to achieve in one generation what it had taken Western countries three centuries to do. But side by side with this progress, there were new troubles. Before Braithwaite left, he read in the Accra papers the text of President Nkrumah's Dawn Broadcast of April 8, 1961, denouncing corruption.

The same men who had worked at Nkrumah's side in pre-Independence days, who had campaigned for him and gone to prison with him, were now living in luxury in palatial mansions, amassing property, riding in fine limousines, flaunting wealth obviously far above their incomes. In the Dawn Broadcast, Nkrumah announced a war on "ostentatious living, vain pride, haughtiness in high places, a contemptuous attitude toward the masses." He spoke of a "new ruling class of self-seekers and careerists," and swore to curb this evil "no matter who is gored."

The broadcast was said to have been inspired by a relative newcomer to government ranks, a Ga lawyer named Tawia Adamafio. Adamafio had opposed the CPP before 1954, and with his fellow Ga, Ako Adjei, had edited a newspaper

describing the CPP as a party of "fooling and thieving."
Both changed sides. Nkrumah did not question their sincerity. He was always ready to welcome converts and trust old
enemies, providing Ghana could use their services. Thus he
had appointed Dr. Danquah, perhaps his severest critic, as
a founder of the Ghana Academy of Science.

Ako Adjei, who had deserted him at the time of the split
with the UGCC, became a cabinet minister. After his "conversion" Adamafio gave every evidence of adoring Nkrumah.
He composed songs in praise of him and made popular such
chants as: "Osagyefo is our Leader, our Father, our Teacher,
our Messiah and the Nation's Fount of Honor." Nkrumah
seems to have accepted these public relation services complacently.

Adamafio became General Secretary of the CPP and later
Minister of State for Presidential Affairs. His rapid rise
caused justified resentment among the old-timers who had
been loyal to Nkrumah from the beginning. Adamafio became
the leading crusader against corruption, wherever it existed.

After the Dawn Broadcast, Nkrumah set up an Investigating Committee to find out where his ministers and party
functionaries were getting their money. Newspapers
launched a campaign against them. Their stories aroused a
great deal of indignation among CPP rank and file and the
common people, who had been asked to tighten their belts
for Ghana.

In September 1951, while the investigation was going on,
a wildcat strike broke out among Sekondi-Takoradi railway
and harbor workers, caused in part by the high living of the
VIPs. Strikes had become almost illegal. The Trade Union
Council, like the United Ghana Farmers' Council, was now
a branch of the CPP. Nkrumah urged trade unionists to remember that they were no longer "struggling against capitalism" and urged them "to shed their colonial character."
Yet the grievances of the strikers were just. An increase in

wages in 1960 had all but been wiped out by increased prices. The Sekondi-Takoradi workers had become bitter against the Trade Union Council, which they considered blind to their interests.

Nkrumah was on an extensive tour of Russia and other Eastern countries when the strike broke out. Komla Gbedemah, Minister of Health, and Kojo Botsio, Minister of Agriculture, pleaded vainly with the strikers to go back to work. Nkrumah, learning about the situation in Belgrade, ordered Tawia Adamafio to handle it.

Like many Ghana intellectuals, Adamafio had little use for the common people. Over the radio he referred to the strikers as rats—"Western rats" by one version, "despicable rats" by another. The strikers were outraged, as were practically all of the nation's workers. Not until Nkrumah returned and intervened personally was the strike ended. Yet he forgave Adamafio his dreadful gaffe.

The Investigating Committee issued a report showing that many party functionaries and government officials had accepted graft, mostly in the form of bribes from foreign firms. When the judiciary took no steps to punish them, Nkrumah asked six of his cabinet ministers to resign, among them Komla Gbedemah and Kojo Botsio, his oldest and most trusted supporters. As a result he was accused of trying to get rid of possible rivals. Botsio was later reinstated, but Gbedemah became openly anti-Nkrumah and shortly afterward left the country.

Krobo Edusei was not asked to resign, although the Investigating Committee had called his conduct "below any acceptable standard for men in the public service." Because of his generosity to those in need, he was one of the most popular of the ministers. People said of him that if he was corrupt, it was from foreigners he took money. Later he became notorious because of a gold-plated bed his wife bought in London "for personal purposes."

After the strike several of its leaders were arrested. Dr. Danquah was detained under the Preventive Detention Act, along with a few other Opposition members. They were not accused of causing the strike, but of encouraging it, providing aid to the strikers, and using the strike to make adverse propaganda abroad.

On August 1, 1962, Nkrumah was returning home after a visit to President Maurice Yaméogo of Upper Volta, a former French colony due north of Ghana. In his party were Tawia Adamafio, Ako Adjei and Coffie Crabbe, another Ga who was a protégé of Adamafio. At Kulungugu, in Ghana, just across the border from Upper Volta, Nkrumah made a last-minute decision to stop. He had got out of his car and was greeting a group of schoolchildren, when someone threw a hand grenade. Nkrumah escaped serious injury, but a school-boy and a policeman were killed, and over fifty others were wounded.

Adamafio, Ako Adjei, and Coffie Crabbe, who usually flanked Nkrumah, were some distance away when the explosion occurred. Since no one outside Nkrumah's party had known in advance of his change of plans, suspicion fell on these three. They were said to be behind a revived Ga tribal movement to assassinate him. Nkrumah himself came to believe in their guilt. (There were stories that he had been told of it by a witch doctor he had consulted.) All three men were arrested and held under the Preventive Detention Act.

The attempted assassination was followed by a series of bombings in Accra. Thirty people were killed, and over three hundred were injured and maimed. At a public meeting the police arrested a man with a concealed grenade. His confession led to the discovery that Obetsebi Lamptey, of the UGCC "Big Six," who had gone to Togo to escape detention, had returned secretly, supplied the grenades and paid the bomb throwers. He was captured and held in preventive detention. Lamptey was found to be suffering from incurable cancer and was transferred to a private ward in the Accra hospital. In spite of the best medical attention available he died soon afterward.

Following Lamptey's arrest and the Accra bombings, Adamafio, Ako Adjei, and Coffie Crabbe were accused of treason and brought to trial. The presiding judge was Sir Arku Korsah, who also served as Chairman of the Presidential Committee of three who administered Ghana when Nkrumah was away. The trial lasted fifty-one days. The court held that the United Party, led by the late Obetsebi Lamptey, had conceived the Kulungugu plot and the Accra bombings. Adamafio was found guilty of "expansive vanity" and "inordinate ambition" and there was some indication that Ako Adjei might have obtained money by false pretenses. However, there was little evidence that Adamafio, Adjei, or Coffie Crabbe were involved in the attempted assassination. On December 9, 1962, all three were acquitted.

Had the trial followed colonial precedent, Sir Arku Korsah, in his capacity as a government official, would have notified Nkrumah in advance that acquittal was likely, and the proceedings would have been halted. As it was, his verdict enraged rank-and-file CPP members, who already resented the high positions given African aristocrats like Sir Arku. Thousands marched in protest demonstrations.

On the grounds that Sir Arku had betrayed his government responsibilities, Nkrumah used the power given him by the constitution to dismiss him as Chief Justice. He was not removed from the Bench and remained a member of the Court of Appeal. Immediately afterward, on Nkrumah's persuasion, the National Assembly, at a special session, passed the Law of Criminal Procedure (Amendment No. 2) Act, which gave the President power to refute any decision of the Special Court. On December 25, on the basis of this act, Nkrumah declared the acquittal verdict null and void. Nkrumah then set up another court with twelve jurors, which brought a verdict of guilty and sentenced the three to death.

The case brought storms of protest against Nkrumah abroad, mostly from people who knew little of the background. At home, his dismissal of Sir Arku Korsah as Chief Justice broke his shaky alliance with the Ghana aristocracy, whose very conservatism lent Ghana respectability in the Western world. Later, on Nkrumah's orders, the three death sentences were commuted to twenty years' imprisonment. Among his critics, his clemency received no praise.

Although Nkrumah was accused abroad of the same luxurious living as his colleagues, his personal tastes were still fairly simple. Aside from his flat in Osu Castle, he had a residence at Flagstaff House in Accra, which he used increasingly after he became President. Flagstaff House was built during the Second World War for the British commander in West Africa. It had been considered too small and undignified for the British governor general. A German journalist called Flagstaff a "Colonial Fort" where the President lived cooped up in fear of his own people behind a heavily armed presidential guard.

The President's Guard was actually the creation of the British Major General H. T. Alexander, who served as Commander of the Ghana Army in 1960 and 1961. Alexander referred to the Guard as "a home for old soldiers unfit for active service." In the Freedom House complex were other buildings used for homes and offices of various state dignitaries. Flagstaff Hall had a wall around it, and there was another ornamental wall around the complex, about waist-high, sufficient only to keep out small boys. Nkrumah never lived in the much more impressive State House, built originally for the governor general. It became a guest house for visiting heads of state.

Nkrumah's working day still stretched into eighteen hours. His colleagues grew accustomed to receiving telephone calls from him on some state matter at two-thirty or four-thirty in the morning. But work never became an obsession with him, and he was capable of dropping everything to chat with a friend or to obey a whim. An American photographer once received permission to photograph Nkrumah at work before a stack of papers in his Flagstaff House office. He did not even look up while the photographer made his films, but when the American was about to leave Nkrumah proposed a game of darts. An aide brought in a dart board, and they played for a couple of hours.

In contrast to his modest private life, his public appearances were increasingly elaborate. He always traveled with a huge retinue, though it was no larger than those of most Western leaders and certainly less than those of many Middle East potentates. A visitor described his arrival before the National Assembly: "his personal herald literally chanting his praises from afar off; his eight linguists with their gold-headed staves."

Many Western writers described Nkrumah's charm, implying that his success was due to charm alone. General Alexander succumbed to that charm. Even after his abrupt dismissal, he said that should Nkrumah ever ask for help again it would not be easy to refuse him. The qualities of charm which Nkrumah had was in a large degree made up of a lively interest in people, a curiosity about everything, a sense of fun, ready laughter, a gracious way, consideration of others in personal relationships. These were not unique qualities among Ghanaians. They are indeed common among African people almost everywhere. It is possible that the European colonists, seeing Africans either as savages or servants, simply overlooked them.

Step by step and always constitutionally, Nkrumah became an absolute ruler. From 1961 to 1966, he was responsible for legislation which turned Ghana into a one-party government, with its President in supreme control of almost every area of life. Some of that legislation, and the reasons for its enactment, have been discussed already. An amendment to the Criminal Code in 1961 made it a criminal offense to do anything that would make the President "an object of hatred, ridicule or contempt." The Preventive Detention Act was extended to allow ten years' detention. The Security Service Act of 1963 placed the Security Service administratively under the President. By the Prisons Act, passed the same year, prisons were placed directly under the President, including the facilities for detainees.

Whether out of loyalty or fear of falling into disfavor, CPP Assembly members supported Nkrumah in everything. The British Government Agents and their superiors, the Regional Officers, were gradually replaced by CPP government appointees who because of a legal complication, took back the old titles of District Commissioners and Regional Commissioners. Their duties entailed supporting government policy, in everything from a mass-inoculation campaign to the promotion of adult education classes. They were more or less judged by the strength of the CPP vote in their areas, which made them prey to the temptation of using undue influence on the voters.

Even many of Nkrumah's long-standing admirers found his one-party state deplorable. It became harder and harder to answer the jibes and jeers of those who had labeled him a tyrant from the beginning. How could one defend someone who allowed no opposition, and who in addition rid his government one after another of men who had once been his closest friends? The Nkrumah of this period answered his critics without hesitation: he did what he had to do to "preserve Ghana's stability." The explanation was hard to accept, especially for those brought up in the atmosphere of Western-style democracy.

On January 2, 1964, a police constable named Seth Ametewee, who was on duty at Flagstaff House, fired five shots at Nkrumah as he was leaving his office for lunch. He missed Nkrumah but killed a police superintendent, Salifu Dagarti, who had tried to disarm him. Seth Ametewee was subsequently tried for the murder of the police superintendent and sentenced to be hanged—the nearest to a "political" execution in Nkrumah's regime.

As a result of this new assassination attempt, there was an investigation of the police department. In large part the department was an inheritance from colonial times, when the main task of the police was to protect their colonial rulers. Nkrumah had long suspected that it harbored enemies of Ghana's independence, but there was little he could do about it until a new police force was trained. The Commissioner of Police, Eric Madjitey, was now replaced by John W. K. Harlley, head of the Special Branch, in whom Nkrumah had great confidence.

Several of the Opposition suspected of complicity in the assassination plot were arrested under the Preventive Detention Act. Among them, Dr. Danquah was detained for the second time. He died in a detention camp on February 4, 1965. Nnamdi Azikiwe, then President of Nigeria, who had known Nkrumah and Danquah since the days when he was a journalist in Accra, wrote a eulogy of him. Although he and Danquah had not seen eye to eye politically, he expressed regret that Danquah had not been tried publicly, told his offense, given an opportunity to defend himself, "and either been discharged or punished according to whether his guilt or innocence was established beyond any shadow of doubt."

Even before he came to power, Nkrumah had made it clear that the hostility between Western and Eastern bloc nations was not Africa's affair. Repeatedly he had said that Ghana would trade with any nation, provided that she could benefit. Yet in the early years of his rule, Nkrumah's dealings were almost exclusively with the West, and several

African Communists or leftists were actually dismissed from the CPP and government posts.

In 1960, he paid his first trip to the Soviet Union and found it a relief to meet none of the criticism that he received from Western Europe. On his return he bought six big Ilyushin airliners and arranged to send four hundred young Ghanaians to Russia to take officers' training. He also purchased twenty-nine Russian fishing trawlers which were manned by a Russian crew. He accepted more aid from the Soviet Union later, in the form of technicians and loans, since he felt that the terms were more advantageous than those he received elsewhere. His "flirtation" with the East was another black mark against him in the Western press.

By the Presidential Election Act of May 1965, only members of the CPP were permitted to be candidates for the presidency. A general election was announced for June 9, 1965, to vote for the National Assembly, which had been increased to 198 members, 10 of them women. On June 2, the government announced that there would be no need to hold the election, that candidates for the president and the assembly nominated by the CPP would automatically be selected. Nkrumah had concluded that an Opposition party was a disruptive nuisance.

At a time when he was belabored by censure abroad and at home, when many of his lifelong friends, both European and African, were turning from him, he could still point with pride to Ghana's progress under the Second Five Year Development Plan.

Whereas in 1951, there were almost no good roads except those for the European gold mines and timber industries, by 1965, Ghana had a network of the most modern roads in Africa. In colonial days, fresh meat, milk, and eggs were available only to Europeans. Through government-subsidized poultry farms and cattle herds, these foods were now becoming part of the Ghanaian diet.

Cocoa had been supplemented by other agricultural products, for export and home consumption. The Workers Brigade had cleared 12,500 acres for the planting of grains and vegetables. On another 24,000 acres, state farms were growing rubber trees, banana trees, coconut palms, palms to produce palm oil, and citrus fruits. Modern farm machinery had increased the productivity of both private and co-operative farms.

The industrial plants completed or nearly so included a steel works, two cocoa-processing plants, two sugar refineries, a textile-printing factory, a glass factory, a chocolate factory, a meat-processing factory, a radio-assembly factory, a factory to manufacture prefabricated houses. An atomic reactor to supply isotopes for medicine and industry was nearly finished. Ghana was beginning to produce its own matches, shoes, nails, rubber tires, cement, asbestos, soft drinks, cigarettes, biscuits, paints, canned fruit, and insecticides. Before Nkrumah, all these goods were imported.

To the colonial Gold Coast's exports of gold and cocoa and timber were added manganese and rough diamonds, of which Ghana had become the world's second-largest producer.

Health centers were functioning in remote areas to serve the rural population. Infant mortality had markedly decreased thanks to maternity and post-natal care centers. The Medical Field Unit had waged an effective campaign against trypanosomiasis, or sleeping sickness. Progress was being made in fighting malaria, leprosy, and tuberculosis, all common diseases in tropical Africa. Five mental hospitals with accommodations for 1,200 patients were scheduled to open in 1970. In 1952, when there were only 45 African doctors in the entire Gold Coast, Nkrumah's government had begun to send youths abroad to study medicine. Many of them were now returning home. A medical school was being built in Ghana. In 1950, the Gold Coast's only nursing school was graduating 8 nurses a year. There were 6 schools of nursing now, graduating an annual average of 265 nurses and trained midwives.

There were phenomenal achievements in the field of education. Primary education was at last free and compulsory for all. Free textbooks were supplied in primary and secondary schools. In 1950, hardly more than 200,000 children were attending primary schools, most of these in the early grades. Now there were nearly 1,500,000. Enrollments in secondary or high schools had increased in the same period from 2,776 students to 35,000. The number of students attending teacher-training colleges had increased from 1,831 in 1950 to an estimated 12,720 by the end of 1965.

Ghana now had two full-fledged universities where there had been none before, the University of Ghana, formerly University College, at Legon, and the Kwame Nkrumah University of Science and Technology. Cape Coast University College was scheduled to acquire full university status in September 1966.

There was also the Kwame Nkrumah Institute of Ideology at Winneba, opened in 1962, which one senior lecturer described as "a cross between Socratic Athens, the London School of Economics and the Moscow Institute of Marxism-Leninism." It was at Winneba that the philosophy of "Nkrumaism" emerged. In essence it reflected Nkrumah's efforts to adapt socialism to the needs of new Africa. Even some of those who most strongly propounded Nkrumaism were often vague about its concepts. It became something of a cult.

Government scholarships supported about 90 per cent of the university students at home and abroad. Ghana desperately needed university men and women trained in the professions, in engineering and agriculture. Nkrumah felt that in return for their education, the young people should be willing to serve their country where their skills were most needed. He did not want them to become gentlemen scholars or "black Englishmen" like the Coastal Elite, contemptuous of the common people. In one broadcast he remarked that the University of Ghana was being turned into "a breeding ground for unpatriotic and anti-Government elements."

Nkrumah took over as chancellor of the university and appointed as his vice-chancellor Conor Cruise O'Brien, formerly an Irish representative at the United Nations. O'Brien objected to turning the university into a political battlefield and more or less openly accused Nkrumah of interfering with academic freedom. After he finished his contract he was not asked to return. He bore Nkrumah no malice. In New York, he was pressured to say that Nkrumah was a fascist, but he refused. Nkrumah was not a fascist, O'Brien maintained: "He was not cruel, or militaristic, or racist."

Ghana had had to borrow heavily for its vast construction projects. Even allowing for some mismanagement because of inexperience and haste, the money had not been wasted. It was an investment for the future. But through no fault of Nkrumah nor his government, two disastrous blows threatened Ghana's economy.

A large part of Ghana's reserves had been lodged in England, as a guarantee of the nation's stability. The English banking concerns in charge of the reserves had made some ill-advised investments. As a result, Ghana was faced with the staggering loss of 60 million pounds.

The other crippling blow was the sudden fall in world cocoa prices. Having survived the swollen shoot disease, cocoa production had increased from 274,000 tons in 1957 to 590,000 tons in 1964. A fall in world cocoa prices from 467 pounds a ton in 1954 to 140 pounds a ton in 1965 more than wiped out the profits. Nkrumah was convinced that Western nations who bought cocoa from Ghana, including some of his fellow Commonwealth countries, had purposely inflicted this economic squeeze.

The two catastrophes meant bad news in the 1966 budget, more taxation, more sacrifices from the common people. Nkrumah still saw the setback as only temporary.

On January 23, 1966, he presided over the inauguration ceremony of the great Volta River Dam project, held at Aksosomba on the Volta, some sixty miles northeast of Accra. His great dream was about to become a reality. To the vast crowd of spectators, among them Ghana's most distinguished citizens, foreign diplomats, foreign investors, and technicians who had worked on the project, he described what it encompassed.

A new hydroelectric power plant, with power supplied by the Volta Dam, was about to be put in operation. Its initial power output would be 512,000 kilowatts, or 588,000 kilowatts at full load. The ultimate power output would be 768,000 kilowatts, or 882,000 kilowatts at full load.

The plant would supply electricity to a large factory at Tema for processing aluminum from bauxite more cheaply than anywhere else in the world. The plant would support many other industries as well and would mean widespread electrification of Ghana and neighboring countries.

The modern harbor and township of Tema on the coast, which were part of the project, were already completed. Water was building up behind the dam to form the largest man-made lake in the world, 250 miles long with a shore-line of 4,500 miles. Approximately 80,000 people had been moved from the area to be submerged. Some of them had been settled on farms and provided with up-to-date equipment for farming and animal husbandry. For the rest, fifty new villages and towns had been built, provided with modern houses, schools, piped water, electricity, medical facilities.

As a reservoir, the lake could supply water to towns and

villages and irrigate farms. The fluctuation of its water level made raising rice possible. It was foreseen as a tourist attraction and vacation spot. Most important was its contribution to the fresh-water fish industry. A great deal of research had been done on which fish to breed to increase the supply and how to control weed growth. Fishing ports were being built around the lake.

The total cost of the Volta River project, including the Tema Harbor, had come to around 105 million pounds, of which Ghana had been able to provide 35 million pounds. Not only was the project expected to repay its foreign investors amply, it was the key to Ghana's future prosperity.

Following Nkrumah's speech there was a moment of silence. Then he turned a switch. Lights went on illuminating the dam, while lights on the bank were switched off to emphasize the contrast. The Volta hydroelectric plant was officially opened.

Afterward, Nkrumah walked through the semi-darkness, greeting people he recognized in the crowd. If there were any security guards near him, they were not in evidence.

11

CHAMPION OF AFRICAN UNITY

The independence of Ghana is meaningless unless it is
linked up with the total liberation of Africa.

—NKRUMAH

Nkrumah had another great dream, African unity. It had
been with him ever since the Fifth Pan-African Congress in
Manchester in 1945 and his subsequent founding of the West
African National Secretariat.

In speech after speech he talked of the need of African
countries to present a united front before independence
against their colonial rulers, and afterward because so
many of the new nations were too poor and small to stand
alone.

He proposed establishing an African Common Market,
similar to the European Common Market, to give Africans
the advantage of free trade among themselves. He constantly
tried to break down the isolation that European powers had
imposed on their African colonies. It was often easier to fly
to Paris or London than to another African state. Letters and
telephone calls went through more quickly to Europe. Roads
and railways built by the colonial rulers stopped within the
boundaries of their own colonies.

Nkrumah also conceived the idea of a federation of African nations, almost as tightly linked as the states in the
United States of America. There were language barriers to
be overcome, caused both by the multiplicity of African

tongues and dialects and the official languages imposed
by European powers. This was only one of many difficulties
involved. Nkrumah considered none of them insurmounta-
ble.

After Ghana became independent, Nkrumah increased his
efforts to bring African states together. In April 1958, he
launched the African-unity movement by calling the First
Conference of Independent States. Eight independent African nations were represented. Only Ghana and Liberia represented the area south of the Sahara. The others were
Egypt, Tunisia, Libya, Sudan, Morocco, which were pre-
dominantly Arabic-speaking and Moslem, and Ethiopia.

Differences in race, color of skin, religion, and language
proved no barrier to agreement on crucial matters. The
conference declared itself unalterably opposed to colonialism, voted to support the struggle for freedom then going
on in Algeria, condemned the apartheid system in South
Africa. They gave their support to the United Nations
Declaration of Human Rights and condemned racialism
among their own people as well as from the outside. They
agreed to settle any disputes, should they arise, by concilia-
tion and mediation within the African community. Toward
what they called "the two antagonistic blocs" of the East
and the West, they adopted a policy of non-alignment.

France, like England, had come to the conclusion that it
was infeasible to hold colonies against their will. That year,
President Charles de Gaulle toured the French territories in
Africa, offering them a choice of independent political existence of membership within the French Community, which
resembled the British Commonwealth. Only Guinea, under
the proud idealist, Sékou Touré, rejected the trade and other
advantages of belonging to the French Community. He
reportedly told de Gaulle that the Guineans preferred
"freedom in poverty to riches in servitude." On October 2,

1958, Guinea became independent, with Sékou Touré as its first President.

De Gaulle was so angered by Touré's stubbornness that he immediately banned French aid to Guinea and recalled all French administrative officers and military units. The colonists left in great haste, took everything they could with them, and attempted to smash what they could not carry. French villas were gutted. Records and files were burned or destroyed. One man spitefully cut the light cords in his garage and chopped up his water hose.

Undisturbed, Sékou Touré set himself to bring order from the shambles. The Soviet Union recognized Guinea on October 5 and offered aid, but recognition from Western nations, including the United States, did not come until considerably later.

In November, Sékou Touré visited Nkrumah in Accra. The two men discovered that they had kindred hopes, kindred dreams. They became friends, "close as brothers." Nkrumah arranged a loan from his government to Guinea of $28,000,000. It was a gesture of solidarity but not of charity. Though the people of Guinea were as poor as those in all colonial countries, Guinea was wealthy in natural resources and had the richest bauxite reserves in the world. On November 23, Nkrumah and Sékou Touré signed an informal agreement "to constitute our two States as the nucleus of a Union of West African States."

Nkrumah took the lead in organizing the first All African Peoples' Conference, held in Accra in December 1958. Delegates came not only from independent African states but from countries still under colonialism. Tom Mboya of Kenya was elected president of the Conference. Julius Nyerere, who would be Tanzania's first Prime Minister, played an active role, as did Dr. Félix Moumie, nationalist party leader in the French Cameroons, and Roberto Holden, who represented Portuguese Angola.

Also present was an intense and eloquent young man named Patrice Lumumba, head and founder of the *Mouvement National Congolais*, the National Congolese Movement, of the Belgian Congo. In education and political development, the Congolese people lagged far behind the Ghanaians. The Belgian administration had always treated them like children. There was no Coastal Elite in the Congo, and not a single Congolese in a high government post. The only Congolese who could study abroad were those sent by missionaries to train as priests or pastors. Lumumba had supplemented his primary school education by correspondence courses, but the best job he could get was as a postal clerk, where he earned a fraction of the pay of his white colleagues. He found the Conference an exciting experience, was somewhat awed by Nkrumah, and was inordinately pleased when this great African leader noticed him.

Some sympathetic Europeans also attended the Conference. Patrick Duncan, grandson of South Africa's first governor, came to represent the South African Liberal Party. He had shown his support of the country's nonwhites, Africans and Indians, by marching side by side with them in their passive resistance campaign. The Reverend Michael Scott, who had been forced to leave South Africa because of his opposition to apartheid, represented the oppressed Herero people of South-West Africa. In his opening address, Nkrumah referred to these Europeans among them: "We welcome into our midst peoples of all other races, other nations, other communities who desire to live among us in peace and equality."

Five months after the Accra Conference, on May 1, 1959, Nkrumah and Sékou Touré met at Conakry, capital of Guinea, to seal their pact. By the Conakry Declaration, they described the Ghana-Guinea Union as the nucleus of a union of independent African states. The union was to have a flag of red, gold, and green, with as many black stars as there were members. No visas would be needed for citizens of the member states. The union was to take the lead in co-ordinating historical research, the teaching of languages, and cultural activities designed "to promote the harmonious development of African civilization."

Nkrumah's friend, President William Tubman of Liberia, was alarmed at the word "union," fearful that it meant African states would lose their own sovereignty. Nkrumah and Sékou Touré met with him for a three-day conference at the Liberian village of Sanniquellie. The result was the Sanniquellie Declaration, which referred to a "Community of Independent States," but tactfully omitted the word "union."

In February 1960, President de Gaulle of France authorized the explosion of an atomic bomb at a test site in the Sahara. There were world-wide protests, including those from both the United States and the Soviet Union, and the test explosion was condemned by the UN General Assembly. In Africa, Nkrumah took the lead in protesting the use of African soil as a nuclear testing ground. His indignation grew when a team of British and Canadian scientists in Ghana reported a substantial increase in radioactivity, thus disproving the French claim that radioactive debris would not be carried more than 700 miles. After the second bomb explosion in the Sahara, Ghana recalled her ambassador to France.

A committee led by the Reverend Michael Scott tried to reach the Sahara testing site but were turned back in the French Upper Volta. On April 7, 1960, Nkrumah proposed that African nations adopt Positive Action to free the continent from further "perils of atomic arrogance." His suggestion was that hundreds of Africans should march to the testing site, risking arrest and imprisonment, as Gandhi's followers had done during the historic Salt March in India. Other nations applauded the idea, but no action was taken.

The Second Conference of Independent African States

was held in Addis Ababa in Ethiopia, on June 15, 1960. In addition to the eight nations that attended the first conference, there were representatives from newly independent Nigeria, Somalia, Sudan, Cameroun (formerly the French Cameroons), and the Algerian Provisional Government. Nkrumah did not attend but sent Ako Adjei, then Ghana's Foreign Minister, to represent Ghana. In his speech Adjei emphasized Nkrumah's long dream of a union of African states: "To us in Ghana the concept of African unity is an article of faith."

His only strong support came from Guinea. Most of the delegates were indifferent. Yussuf Maitma Sule, leader of the Nigerian delegation, commented that while Pan-Africanism was the only solution to Africa's problems, the idea of forming a union was "premature." "If anybody makes the mistake of feeling that he is a Messiah who has got a mission to lead Africa," he said, "the whole purpose of Pan-Africanism will, I fear, be. defeated." This remark was clearly a slap at Nkrumah, and subsequently relations between Ghana and Nigeria became strained.

There were other disagreements among the Addis Ababa delegates, but they were unanimous in adopting resolutions to ban nuclear tests in Africa, to eradicate colonial rule, and to oppose apartheid and racial discrimination.

The year 1960 was an eventful one in Africa. Counting the island of Madagascar, sixteen African nations became independent and were made members of the United Nations. Among them was the former Belgian Congo, which became the Democratic Republic of the Congo on June 30, 1960, with Patrice Lumumba as Prime Minister.

Nkrumah had taken a paternal interest in Lumumba ever since the 1958 Accra Conference. Now he was worried. Belgium's decision to grant independence to her colony had been abrupt. Almost nothing had been done to prepare the new African leaders for their administrative duties. The

Congo was one of the largest African states and among the very richest. From the province of Katanga came enormous amounts of copper, cobalt, uranium, and other minerals. Kasai Province supplied 80 per cent of the world's industrial diamonds. There was gold in Kivu Province. Nkrumah foresaw that Belgian and other industrialists who had profited by this great wealth were not going to relinquish it readily.

Five days after the Congo's independence, a mutiny broke out in the Congolese army, sparked by their Belgian commander, General Émile Janssens, an arrogant racist who told his Congolese soldiers: "In the army the whites will remain superior to the blacks." Lumumba, with the Congo's President, Joseph Kasavubu, personally toured the mutinous areas and within a couple of days had to a large measure restored order.

But greatly exaggerated stories of atrocities against Europeans spread rapidly. Almost overnight there was a mass exodus. The new government was bereft of its badly needed white civil servants, doctors, magistrates, technicians.

On July 10, Belgian parachutists landed in Katanga. Other landings followed. Belgians took over the airport of Leopoldville, the capital. With a still unexplained brutality, Belgian planes strafed Matadi, on the Lower Congo River, while a Commando ship fired on the town. Some sixty civilians were killed. The Belgian actions undid Lumumba's efforts to restore order. Soldiers turned mutinous again, convinced that Belgium was taking back their independence. On July 11, Moise Tshombe, a devoted friend of the white industrialists, announced the secession of mineral-rich Katanga Province.

Lumumba and Kasavubu appealed for military aid from the United Nations on July 12, charging that Belgium had violated their Treaty of Friendship by landing troops without the consent of the Congolese government. The UN Security Council promptly voted to supply that aid. Nkrumah, in the name of Ghana, was the first African head of state to offer help to Lumumba, and in a telephone call to UN Secretary General Hammarskjöld repeated his offer.

On July 15, the first UN troops were flown to the Congo, one contingent from Tunisia and another from Ghana, all wearing blue berets, the insignia of UN military forces. Troops from India, Sweden, and Ireland joined them later, but the UN forces lacked the authority and equipment to stop the holocaust that swept the Congo: the secession of Kasai, the province of diamonds; the outbreak of tribal warfare; the razing of African villages by Tshombe's white mercenaries; the mass starvation; the dissolution of the Lumumba government; the military coup of General Joseph Mobutu; Lumumba's death by torture on January 17, 1961; Hammarskjöld's own mysterious death the following September in a plane crash on his way to Rhodesia to try to reason with Tshombe.

Throughout the tragic Congo drama, Nkrumah pursued his efforts to bring peace. He called a Conference of Independent African States at Leopoldville on August 25, 1960, but while the other nations were content to let the United Nations handle the situation, Nkrumah did not hesitate to give Secretary General Hammarskjöld the benefit of his advice. He wrote Lumumba to keep calm. He pleaded with the intractable Moise Tshombe to stop co-operating with the imperialists who "will discard you as soon as you have served their purpose." His correspondence reflects a certain amount of egotism; he is so positive he is right. Yet in view of what transpired later, it is hard not to conclude there would have been less bloodshed had people listened to him more attentively.

Though Nkrumah was free with advice, he did not attempt to interfere with UN military tactics, even when Ghanaian troops were assigned to guard the Leopoldville radio station to prevent Patrice Lumumba from telling his side of the story. The Ghanaian contingent, which had been with the Tunisians the first to reach the Congo, were the last Africans to leave.

The Congo tragedy had the unfortunate side effect of splitting the African heads of state into pro- and anti-Lumumbists. The leaders of former French colonies now independent, but unlike Guinea still within the French Community, met several times in Brazzaville, capital of the former French Congo. Most of them took a stand against the Lumumba government.

The Casablanca Conference was held between January 3 and 7, 1961, by Ghana, Guinea, Mali, the three North African countries, Morocco, Egypt, and Libya, and one non-African nation, Ceylon. The seven had in common that their governments supported Patrice Lumumba and in their resolution on the Congo they urged the United Nations to restore his "legitimate Government of the Republic of the Congo" and to "disarm and disband the lawless bands of Mobutu." (Within a few days Lumumba would be murdered; Mobutu is still President of the Congo, renamed the Zaïre.)

In July, the Guinea-Ghana Union was enlarged to include Mali, under President Modibo Keita. He met in Accra with Nkrumah and Sékou Touré to discuss a closer co-operation of their countries, politically, economically, and culturally. Both Touré and Keita felt that military aid should be sent to the Congolese government-in-exile, set up in Stanleyville by followers of Lumumba, but Nkrumah thought this would be futile. A few other disagreements marred their meetings. They did resolve that each of their three nations should have a Resident Minister serving in the cabinets of the other two; the arrangement never worked out successfully. Nor could Nkrumah persuade other nations to join their Union.

Though his plan for a tightly knit federation of African states never materialized, his constant call for unity made his colleagues realize that some sort of coalition was necessary. At Addis Ababa, in May 1963, the Organization of African Unity was formed. The word "unity" was inserted to conciliate Nkrumah, to whom it had meant so much for so long. At this meeting, independent African states resolved actively to support liberation struggles in the Portuguese colonial territories, and in South-West Africa, South Africa, and Southern Rhodesia. It was also resolved to receive and train freedom fighters from these regions. That violence would be necessary to liberate these last strongholds of colonialism was at last accepted as inevitable.

Nkrumah went ahead on his own to carry out the OAU program to aid guerrillas. Ghana became a symbol of freedom to refugees from colonial rule. A camp was set up at Monkrong under a team of Russian instructors, to train freedom fighters in machine-gunnery, rocket-launching, the firing of mortars. When Rhodesia's white government declared itself independent in 1965, Nkrumah took a strong stand against Britain, which had declared embargoes on what it called the illegal regime and deplored the plight of the black majority, but failed to enact more forceful measures. Nkrumah did not, however, threaten to send Ghanaian troops to Rhodesia, as his enemies claimed. His only military intervention in his career was to send troops to the Congo under UN supervision.

Since its inception in 1963, the Organization of African Unity has become an integral part of independent Africa. It has had impact both in international conferences and within the United Nations. As a result of OAU pressure, the UN Security Council in August 1963 went beyond condemning South Africa for apartheid practices, which they had done for years, and called on UN member governments to halt the sales of arms, ammunition, and military vehicles to South Africa. The OAU also called on South Africa to release its political prisoners.

The greatest danger facing emerging Africa, as Nkrumah

saw it, was a phenomenon of post World War II years, which he called "neo-colonialism." Neo-colonialism began when Western powers realized that there was an easier way to make money out of Africa than through running colonies— simply to pull out and leave the Africans in charge, eliminating all the expenses of colonial administration. Since the new black leaders were mostly inexperienced and sometimes naïve in financial matters, the Western powers were as free as ever to make money out of their former colonies.

In 1965, Nkrumah wrote *Neo-Colonialism, Last Stage of Imperialism*, a thoroughly researched work which exposed the huge and interlinking industrial monopolies in Africa and described how they operated to gain control of the continent's gold, diamonds, and other wealth. The book did not make him more popular in the Western world. After its publication the United States State Department summoned the Ghanaian chargé d'affaires in Washington and made a formal protest. Reportedly, a promised U.S. aid program to Ghana was canceled because of the book. No charges were made that its accusations were incorrect. Much of the book's contents had indeed been printed elsewhere, including financial publications such as the *Wall Street Journal*.

Also in 1965, the last OAU meeting Nkrumah attended was held in Accra. Nkrumah was determined to make it so impressive that the whole world would take notice. Accra was transformed into a "showplace for African unity." Flower beds sprang up almost overnight all over the city. OAU flags festooned every street corner. Outside Nkrumah's Flagstaff House residence were portraits of the thirty-six heads of state expected.

To house the delegates and other guests, a complex of buildings was erected on the State House grounds. The residential unit was a twelve-story modern apartment house. The conference hall, equipped with facilities for simultaneous interpreting, was built to hold a thousand people. The banquet hall had space for two thousand. All three buildings, air-conditioned throughout, were linked by covered passageways. Two large fountains soared sixty feet high while multi-colored lights played on them.

The total cost of these new facilities approached eight million pounds and has been cited as the supreme example of Nkrumah's extravagance. Yet, with the project's completion, Accra became the only city south of the Sahara where full-scale international conferences could be held. International conferences are considered an excellent basis from which to launch an extensive tourist industry.

Nkrumah's dedication to unity extended beyond the limits of Africa, to include all countries which had suffered under colonialism. He had great sympathy for Vietnam, which had been colonized by the French, conquered by the Japanese during the Second World War, and which, in his opinion, had then become a victim of American neo-colonialism. On February 21, 1966, a few weeks after the Volta Dam ceremonies, he left for Hanoi, on the invitation of the late North Vietnamese President, Ho Chi Minh. With him he took peace proposals. It was his hope that since he had lived under colonialism on the other side of the world, he would be able to offer objective advice.

Among the officials at the airport to see him off were John W. K. Harlley, Police Commissioner since the Flagstaff House assassination attempt, who in Nkrumah's words had "treason and treachery" in his mind, and Major General Charles Barwah, Deputy Commander of the Ghana Army, whom he would never see again. As he shook hands with them, both wished him a good journey.

In Nkrumah's party were twenty-two government officials, among them Alex Quaison-Sackey, former president of the UN Security Council, who was now Foreign Minister, and sixty-six other personnel, security officers, and Nkrumah's personal secretariat. After brief stops in Egypt and Rangoon, they flew to Peking, from which they planned to take off for Hanoi.

Prime Minister Chou En-lai and other leading Chinese officials met them at the airport. They were driven to the Government House, where they were to stay. Nkrumah retired to his room to rest after the long flight. The Chinese ambassador to Ghana knocked at his door.

"Mr. President, I have bad news," he said on entering. "There has been a coup d'état in Ghana." Later Nkrumah learned that the Chinese welcoming party knew that his government had been overthrown when they greeted him at the airport, but they had courteously refrained from mentioning it so that he could be told privately.

Nkrumah attended a state banquet in his honor that night but canceled all other engagements. He knew now that he could not go to Hanoi. He must return to Africa as soon as possible. In the next days messages of support came from many countries, including some who had criticized him severely at one time or another. Several African nations offered him immediate hospitality. He accepted the invitation from his "brother," President Sékou Touré of Guinea.

Most of his official colleagues, including Foreign Minister Quaison-Sackey, left on one pretext or another. A good part of them returned to Ghana to offer their services to the new government. Nkrumah's security officers and personal staff stayed with him. They reached Guinea on March 2 and were welcomed with a twenty-one-gun salute. At a mass rally in Conakry the next day, President Touré announced that Kwame Nkrumah had been made his co-head of state. Nkrumah, who knew little French, was not aware of the honorary title bestowed him until afterward.

Within days he had arranged an efficient communications systems with persons inside Ghana, so he that could learn what had happened and what was going on in his country.

12

THE MILITARY COUP

President Nkrumah's revolutionary work cannot be replaced, and we do not accept that some music comedy general, helped by policemen, should question the Ghanaian people's twenty years of struggle.

— Foreign Minister OUSMANE BA, of Mali

According to one of the conspirators, Major Akwasi Afrifa, the Ghana coup was the brainchild of his superior officer, Colonel E. K. Kotoka. Afrifa tells his version of the affair in his book, *The Ghana Coup,* a curious mixture of schoolboy English and erudite phraseology that seems to bear the stamp of the Coastal Elite.

Early in February 1966, Afrifa says, he accompanied Colonel Kotoka to Tamale and Yendi in the Northern Territories on training maneuvers. Kotoka became quite friendly with him and confided that he "disliked the Convention People's Party intensely, and the way our army was being run." Afrifa was "happy and elated" that Colonel Kotoka had expressed such trust in him. On their way back from maneuvers, they discussed plans by which Kwame Nkrumah's government could "be toppled by force of arms," although at that time they "were talking vaguely."

A few days later, Afrifa visited Kotoka's home and they "conversed" about Nkrumah's forthcoming visit to Hanoi and agreed that a coup should be staged during his absence. "He [Kotoka] was so happy that we stayed up till the early hours of the morning, drinking beer and making plans." The next morning Kotoka went to Accra to see Nkrumah's trusted Commissioner of Police, John W. K. Harlley, to enlist his support, which he apparently gave willingly. Afrifa claims that so far as he knew they were the only ones thus far to know about the plan. They decided that Major General Ankrah should head the new government but did not tell him about it.

On Nkrumah's orders, General Ankrah, with Major General Otu, had been retired from the Army the year before. No charges had been made against them. Both had been given high posts in Accra banks. Afrifa was indignant about the retirements: "This was not the way to treat Generals." He was shocked that Ankrah had not taken "some military action to extricate himself from this humiliation" at the time he was retired. He admits he knew little about General Otu except that he smoked cigars in public, of which he disapproved.

Afrifa, born in Ashanti in 1936, was a personable young man who had taken officer training at the British academy at Sandhurst, where he boasts of having had so many punishment drills that his study timetable had to be larger than average to write them in. Still he looked back on Sandhurst with nostalgia. He calls it, "an institution that teaches that all men are equal," something that has not often been said about any British military academy. He confesses that he is a great admirer of the British way of life and calls Britain "the home of democracy." Nowhere in the pages of his book does he say that there was anything undemocratic about British colonial rule.

Kotoka was quite unknown at the time of the coup. Nkrumah remembered him as the one officer who was late when he came to Flagstaff House to take his oath of allegiance. General Charles Barwah had once accused him of putting his Ewe tribal interests above his military duties.

Harlley, who was born in the Volta region in 1919, had attended the Metropolitan Police College in Hendon, England. A brochure put out about the coup leaders later described him as a man "of a quiet disposition, considerate, kind-hearted, but very firm," who "enjoys the sight and sound of water, but hates to see fire or anything connected with burning." He was married and had eight children.

General Ankrah, who was allegedly not informed in advance of the coup, had been decorated for bravery in the Congo and was a well-known figure. The same brochure says that he was trained at the Officer Cadet Training Unit in Britain, that he was a "keen sportsman" in his school days, that his hobbies were "gardening, films and an occasional swim," and that he was "companionable, friendly and full of good humour."

None of the conspirators had any experience in administration, nor any training outside their military and police activities. It seems hardly possible that they would have taken over a government unless some outside help was promised them. In one passage in his book, Afrifa hints at such a possibility. Colonel Kotoka had made "all the necessary contacts and arrangements," he writes, for a "full-scale military operation lasting for a considerable period."

The inference is clear that some foreign nation was backing them, but so far there have been only guesses as to what country would most profit by Ghana's overthrow. Suspicion has fallen on the United States Central Intelligence Agency, mainly because of Andrew Tully's statement, in his book *C.I.A.: The Inside Story*, that the CIA was responsible for General Mobutu's coup in the Congo.

The "full-scale military operation lasting for a considerable period" was not necessary. The plan got off on schedule. On the morning of February 23, a six-hundred-man garrison at Tamale received orders to move south. A convoy of thirty-five vehicles carried them first to Kumasi and then on to Accra. Major Afrifa took over en route.

Most of the soldiers were from the Northern Territories

and were illiterate. They had been trained to obey their superiors, which they did. In explanation, they were told that Nkrumah intended to send them to fight in Rhodesia and in Vietnam. They were also told that Nkrumah had fled from Ghana with eight million pounds, that there was no government left, and that it was their duty to maintain law and order. Other wild rumors were circulated among them. By one account, to make these contradictory tales more plausible, they were given an issue of hemp (marijuana).

In Accra, in the meantime, Kotoka and Harlley informed General Ankrah that he was to head a revolt. They had judged their man well. He offered no objections.

Early on February 24, Kotoka and a force of twenty-five burst in on Major General Barwah and told him to surrender or join them. Barwah, a man of high character, refused to do either. In the presence of his wife and children, Kotoka shot him down. He was the first casualty.

Other troops went to arrest Brigadier Hasan, Head of Military Intelligence, and Colonel Zanerigu, Commander of the President's Guard. Hasan was seized, but Zanerigu escaped through a window of his home and raced to Flagstaff House to give an alarm. At the same time, the Accra police, on the orders of Commissioner of Police Harlley, were arresting most of the Cabinet ministers and parliament members.

At 5 A.M., Major Afrifa, in a Command Rover, headed a convoy to attack Flagstaff House. Because of Colonel Zanerigu's warning, the elderly soldiers of the President's Guard were ready for them. The rebels suffered their first and almost only casualties.

Another detail took over control of the radio station at 5:25 A.M. At 6 A.M., Colonel Kotoka went on the air to make his announcement:

> Fellow citizens of Ghana, I have come to inform you that the military, in cooperation with the Ghana Police,

have taken over the government of Ghana. The myth surrounding Nkrumah has been broken. Parliament is dissolved and Kwame Nkrumah is dismissed from office. All ministers are also dismissed. The Convention People's Party is disbanded with effect from now. It will be illegal for any person to belong to it.

At Flagstaff House, the President's Guard was still resisting bravely, though they were heavily outnumbered. Their position became hopeless, but they yielded only when their attackers threatened to blow up Nkrumah's residence where his wife and three small children were staying.

Madame Nkrumah, the President's Egyptian wife, was awakened by the shots. She opened the shutters and saw one of the guards lying on the ground. Rushing to the radio, she heard the announcement of the military takeover. She roused her children and their nurse, then telephoned the Egyptian embassy, where she was told the ambassador would do what he could. Almost immediately troops broke into her room and ordered her and the children outside. She was wearing her nightrobe and was given no time to dress.

The children, the nurse, and Madame Nkrumah were first taken to a military camp and an hour later were put in an armored truck and delivered to the Accra police headquarters. They were searched and Madame Nkrumah in her own words was "subjected to rudeness." After that they were driven to the airport and put on a United Airlines plane for Cairo. Soldiers came on board at the last moment and ordered the nurse to stay in Accra. An Egyptian woman passenger loaned Madame Nkrumah some clothes so she could look presentable for her arrival. Her mother, accompanied by representatives of President Nasser, met her at the airport.

Nkrumah's mother, who was eighty and almost blind, was also at Flagstaff. Soldiers made her leave and told her to go where she belonged. Friends took her in and later escorted her to Nkroful, Nkrumah's birthplace, which during his rule had become a place of pilgrimage. Subsequently the house where he was born was burned.

Within the Flagstaff compound, troops dashed from room to room, smashed furniture, ripped out telephones. Nkrumah's office was wrecked and much of his library destroyed. All of his personal papers were confiscated. He never found out what happened to the notes for a history of Africa which he had been compiling for years. None of his personal possessions was returned to him.

The soldiers went on to the Kanda Estate, where a number of security officers were quartered, tossed grenades into the compounds, ransacked the houses and apartments, carried off radios, refrigerators, and other property, shot anyone who tried to stop them. Children were struck with rifle butts. Rank and file police, who knew nothing of what was going on, tried to stop them. There was some fighting between police and troops.

On the streets were scenes of dreadful brutality. Soldiers drunk with liquor they had looted, perhaps on top of marijuana, went on a rampage. At least two parliament members were killed, and others were wounded. An air hostess was shot down on her way to the airport. A market woman who refused to surrender a picture of Nkrumah hanging over her stall was also murdered. From his informants, Nkrumah estimated the total casualties of that day at about 1,600 dead and many more injured. It may have been less—or more.

Detention camps were opened, and all the prisoners held under the Preventive Detention Act were released, a total of 788 rather than the "thousands" Nkrumah had reputedly been holding. About half of these were "gangsters" whom Nkrumah had agreed to detain only because of the entreaties of the police, who claimed they could not cope with them under the normal processes of law. The criminals contributed their share to the disturbances, sometimes entering bars and demanding beer at gunpoint.

Newspapers abroad were prompt to give headlines to the coup, but the violence, murder, and torture that went with it passed almost unnoticed. The American ambassador to Ghana reported, in innocence or ignorance, that it was "bloodless." The general impression given was that the common people of Ghana were rejoicing. Reports emanating from the coup leaders were taken as the undisputed truth. The usually careful New York *Times* reported that "jubilant Ghanaians demolished the twenty-foot-high bronze statue that Nkrumah had erected of himself in Accra."

In fact, the grounds in front of the parliament building, where the statue stood, were cordoned off by the military to keep out unauthorized persons. The day after the coup a demolition truck moved in and the crew tore down the statue. Afterward several photographs were released to the press. One showed several weeping children sitting on the headless statue. Another was of women carrying away chunks of the statue on their heads—from a rear view. Nkrumah suspected that the figures in the photograph were soldiers dressed up as women. Or they might have been Accra's market women, once Nkrumah's strongest supporters, who had a grudge against him because his Abraham Commission had condemned them for profiteering.

Another photograph released shows some Ghanaian women carrying placards with the slogans: "Long Live New Ghana!" "Down with the Tyrant!" "No More Comrades!" and "Check Income of Ministers." Did the market women make these signs themselves on such short notice? Two days later there was an abortive coup in Uganda. After it was put down, Uganda government investigators found placards with similar wording, already lettered and ready for distribution. It seems stretching a point to dismiss the similarity as mere coincidence.

On February 26, the people of Ghana were informed that a "National Liberation Council" had been established and that the council was the new government. The NLC henceforth had full powers to make and issue decrees "which shall have the full force of law in Ghana" and to appoint committees to administer their state affairs. General Ankrah was Chairman of the NLC. Police Commissioner Harlley was Deputy Chairman. There were six other members: Kotoka, Afrifa, and A. K. Ocran, all army officers; B. A. Yajubu, J. E. Nunoo, and A. K. Deku, all in the police force.

Although the people of Accra were certainly not as "jubilant" as the Western world was being told to believe, there were no mass demonstrations against the military and police regime, no popular uprisings. Nkrumah's masses kept silent. They may have hoped that any change would put an end to high prices and higher taxes. They may have become cynical because of the lavish living style of the Very Important People. They may have been afraid. There was no citizens' militia in Ghana. Ghanaians had not had to fight for independence as Americans had once fought for theirs. They were ill-prepared to battle with the usurpers.

There were some demonstrations against Nkrumah in Accra, which, staged or not, were fairly gruesome. In one parade grotesque and obscene effigies of the "Osagyefo" were carried to mock burials in Christian cemeteries. Only the Methodists protested witchcraft's takeover of Christianity. The reaction of people in rural areas when they heard the news was not recorded.

On March 3, Sir Edward Sears, Chairman of the British-controlled Ashanti Goldfields, asked for an interview with General Ankrah, which was granted immediately. According to his report to Ashanti Goldfields shareholders, there were indications that the "new regime" would be "much more satisfactory to deal with than the old." The next day

Britain, the United States, West Germany, and Israel gave official recognition to the National Liberation Council.

Mass arrests continued in the next weeks. In addition to ministers and members of parliament, all officials of the CPP and its associate organizations, including the Trade Union Council, were arrested, as were branch CPP officers throughout the country. Professor Kojo Abraham, vice-chancellor of the University of Ghana, an Oxford Fellow and former governor of the School of Oriental and African Studies in London, was seized, beaten, and thrown unconscious into a police van. The manuscript of a book he was writing was publicly burned along with other books the new regime had decided to ban.

Attorney General Geoffrey Bing was warned by a friend that he and his wife were likely to be killed if the soldiers found them. They took temporary refuge in the Australian High Commission. When the NLC issued a formal demand for his arrest, Bing surrendered, knowing that the publicity surrounding his capture was guarantee against murder. Soldiers tortured him until a commander of the Ghana Navy arrived on the scene and stopped them. He was then put in a prison cell with eleven other white political prisoners and criminals. Curiously enough, laws of segregation were followed, as in colonial times. Eventually he was deported with only the small change he had in his pocket at the time of his arrest. His savings, invested in Ghanaian bonds, were confiscated.

In that first period a vast campaign of slander and abuse was launched against Nkrumah. Before it was certain where he was, a London tabloid had him fleeing to some island with a bevy of pretty girls. The new government invited public inspection at Flagstaff House of what they called "Kwame Nkrumah's juju"—a dead woman and child in a refrigerator, possibly victims of the February 24 massacre.

The inspection was stopped when its managers found out that visitors were coming to Flagstaff on a sort of pilgrimage.

Many Western newspapers printed unconfirmed stories about Nkrumah. He was said to have amassed a fortune of two and a half million pounds by one source and fifty-two million pounds by another. It was stated as "common knowledge" that he was one of the world's largest holders of hidden foreign assets. He was accused of running a gambling casino, of having built luxurious palaces for himself, and of giving expensive gifts from state monies to his favorites, including women. The London *Times* published a photograph of a beautiful girl sitting in a Thunderbird. According to the caption, it was a present from Nkrumah which the NLC had confiscated. Stories were spread about his many mistresses and his even more numerous illegitimate children.

On February 28, the London *Times* gave this description of Flagstaff House:

> There are underground passages running for some miles. These are stocked with more ammunition than that possessed by the whole Ghana Army and with food for something like six months for the 1000 security men in and around Flagstaff House—including an unknown number of Russians and Chinese.

The legend of the tunnel apparently originated with the conspirators. It was one of the many stories they fed their credulous soldiers; they had it stretching to the Accra airport, with Russians arriving through it. Several days after the coup, Kotoka and Afrifa appeared on the Ghana television. While talking about their easy success, one of them said, "And you know, we didn't find any Russians at all—not one! Nor could we find any trace of that tunnel." They both burst out laughing.

The London *Daily Telegraph* claimed to have discovered that Nkrumah had never attended Lincoln University or received any degrees, ignoring completely his much publicized and much photographed return to get his honorary doctor of laws degree.

It is impossible to prove or disprove many of these calumnies, or even to establish if there is an element of truth in them. Geoffrey Bing found that when he told people in London that Nkrumah had built no palaces for himself, they simply would not believe him. The NLC set up various commissions of inquiry allegedly to expose misconduct in their predecessors, and some persons brought before them had reason to implicate Nkrumah to save themselves. Thus Krobo Edusei told one of the commissions that Nkrumah had asked him to take gold bars to Cairo. Nkrumah certainly had easier and safer ways to transfer funds to Cairo, had he so desired.

Nor have his "hidden foreign assets" been discovered. The conspirators found his will among his personal papers. It bequeathed everything he had to the Convention People's Party. The NLC let it be published—a dubious ethical action—but did not release that part of it which listed his financial holdings. Their reticence seems curious, unless the listing revealed that he did not have an enormous fortune and that it was not invested abroad. Nkrumah himself says that what money he had was invested in Ghana.*

The charges that Nkrumah must have found the hardest to bear were those that ridiculed his social and industrial projects. It was said that his primary schools had to depend on Russian teachers who could not speak English, that his cocoa silos were useless because the cocoa beans were sure to split when dropped into them, that his meat canning and leather factories were inoperative because Ghana did not have enough cows, that breweries had licenses for hops but not for malt and so could not produce beer. Every error of

---

* After Nkrumah's death it was found he had left an estate in England and Wales of 6,250 pounds net.

judgment he ever made was magnified, but probably many more were fabricated. His attackers consistently ignored his numerous achievements.

Ever since Nkrumah had been in power, he had had to endure criticism. The barrage of character defamation which flowed from the propaganda machine of the four soldiers and four policemen who had taken over Ghana had a different quality. It gave all the world's racists, all those who had sneered at the desire of Africans to rule themselves, a chance to say "I told you so." On the eve of Independence, Nkrumah had said that the failure of Ghana would have tragic consequences for other African territories. His prophecy had proved all too true.

13

EXILE

Knowledge is proud that he has learn'd so much;
Wisdom is humble that he knows no more.
—WILLIAM COWPER (a favorite quotation of Nkrumah)

Conakry, where Nkrumah lived after the coup, is a city on an island, linked with the mainland by a causeway. Flowering trees and coconut palms line the streets. The surrounding beaches are within walking distance of almost any part of the city. Offshore are several other islands, one of which is said to have been the model for Robert Louis Stevenson's *Treasure Island*.

It was like being in another world, strange and exotic. Guinea had more Moslems than Ghana, and some men still wore red fezzes and long white robes. Women wore wide flaring skirts, short mantles of embroidered gauze, and headgear of brightly patterned cotton tied with wide points on each side.

The ramshackle schools were crowded. A huge effort was being made to wipe out illiteracy. Teachers had come from the French West Indies, as well as from Czechoslovakia and Yugoslavia, sometimes with interpreters who could translate their lessons into French.

Except for the massive silhouette of the Exhibition Building, built by Chinese construction workers, there was little of the modernization so marked in Accra. The French had built it as a French city, their villas with shuttered windows set in gardens of bougainvillea and blooming hibiscus. Even the irate departure, after Sékou Touré opted for independence outside of the French Community, had not destroyed its Old World charm.

Ordinary people, too poor to buy books, kept remarkably well informed on world affairs. They were always ready to launch into an analysis of the Congo situation, the struggle of Guyana in South America for its freedom, or the absurdity of the Eastern and Western blocs trying to embroil Africa in their disputes.

In this novel atmosphere, Nkrumah relaxed, as much as one of his temperament could. For the first time in years his time was his own. He caught up with his reading, especially the latest books on politics, history, science, and philosophy. He played tennis, went for long walks, took daily lessons in French.

From his seaside villa he could see the shores of independent Sierra Leone. In the opposite direction was Portuguese Guinea, where a fierce battle for liberation was under way. He could not see Ghana, but its fate was never far from his mind. A few refugees trickled through. Some still bore marks of beatings from soldiers or police.

In the beginning he broadcast regularly over the Conakry radio to his people. "Arise and organize," he told them. "Let organization be your watchword. Organize in the country; organize in your homes; organize in your workshops, in factories, in farms; organize in your schools, colleges and universities; organize where you may be; organize now and arise in your mass strength and overthrow these traitors and renegades . . ."

All his messages bore the same theme. His informants told him that the Ghanaians tuned in on him secretly, inviting neighbors in to listen, and passed on the things he said by word of mouth. The National Liberation Council was making every effort to stop people from listening, even to confiscating radios. His broadcasts were also heard in other African nations; he received letters about them from Sierra Leone, Gambia, Nigeria, and even South Africa.

As time went on, and the NLC became more firmly entrenched, Nkrumah limited his broadcasts to specific occasions. Thus when a story was spread that he had resigned as President of Ghana, he went on the air to deny it. He was still their President, he assured his people.

A meeting of the Organization of African Unity was scheduled in Addis Ababa in November 1966, the second one that Nkrumah had missed. The Guinea delegation of nineteen, headed by their Foreign Minister, took a Pan-American plane to the Accra airport, where they were to transfer to another plane for Addis Ababa. Ghanaian military arrested all of them, on the excuse that eighty-one Ghana citizens were being held in Guinea against their will. The eighty-one were all in Nkrumah's entourage, those who had gone with him to Peking and others who had joined him in Conakry.

President Sékou Touré was so outraged that he refused to attend the Addis Ababa conference so long as the Ghana NLC delegation was seated. NLC delegates were hissed and booed. The affair caused such a scandal that the NLC was forced to release the Guineans.

A three-man OAU mission went to Conakry to interview the eighty-one Ghanaians. They talked to each one privately, saying that if they wished they would be escorted by plane back to Ghana under a safe conduct agreement. All eighty-one rejected the offer, not only because of loyalty to Nkrumah but because they were distrustful of the NLC's concern for their welfare. In Ghana, their names had been circulated as "wanted persons." If they returned they had good·reason to suspect that they would be imprisoned and perhaps executed. In an open letter to the "NLC clique," they reiterated their allegiance to the constitutional government of Ghana "under the able, wise and progressive leadership of Osagyefo President Kwame Nkrumah."

Although at the beginning of Guinea's independence, Sékou Touré had had to rely for help on the Eastern bloc countries and China, he was now accepting assistance from Western sources. Guinea's enormous bauxite reserves were being developed with loans from the United States and the World Bank.

Newspapers abroad frequently hinted that Nkrumah's presence was an embarrassment to President Touré because of his alliances with Western nations. Evidence points to the contrary. During the 1966 Army Day celebrations, Nkrumah, in a paratrooper's uniform, stood next to Sékou Touré on the platform of the crowded stadium. His Ghanaian entourage marched side by side with the Guineans and were given a rousing ovation. As honorary head of state, Nkrumah appeared with the Guinea President at all state occasions.

In small ways and big ones he was made to feel at home. The Guinean Chief Protocol Officer, Monsieur Sana Camara, was put in charge of his household. His Guinean household and office staff were loyal and devoted, as were the soldiers and police who guarded his residence. The security measures were necessary. In NLC Ghana, he had become Number One on the wanted list. A large reward was offered for his capture, living or dead. His picture was posted everywhere together with his "criminal" record, which ironically included his 1950 prison sentence for his part in the Positive Action campaign.

High Guinea officials, including the President, frequently dined with Nkrumah. Madame Andrée Sékou Touré, the President's wife, was sometimes present. There were guests every day. Diplomats from foreign embassies in Guinea came to pay their respects. There were visits from freedom fighters he had once helped, leaders of progressive organizations, old friends from all over Africa and from abroad.

Geoffrey Bing paid him a visit in July 1967. Nkrumah looked years younger than he had in Ghana, his former Attorney General reported. He gave the impression of a university professor on sabbatical leave. Much of his reading was now done in French, in which he had become proficient. He played chess in the evenings, and he had continued his hobby of growing roses. His guest counted twenty-one species of rosebushes on his terrace, each carefully labeled with its name and the date of planting.

His correspondence was enormous. A postman in London, "married and with one child," offered to come fight for his safe return to Ghana. A German-speaking Swiss said that he had admired Nkrumah for twenty years and that the military takeover of Ghana was "a destestably insidious action."

"Millions of us Black Americans were sick and hurt over your recent ouster from Ghana," read a letter from Chicago, Illinois. "Your great book on Neo-Colonialism is like a candle-light in a dark celler," wrote an ex-paratrooper from Las Vegas, Nevada, whose great-great-great-grandfather had been kidnaped from West African shores many years before.

Similar letters poured in from all over the world.

While Nkrumah welcomed friends and those who came to him for advice and help, he avoided the press. Foreign journalists besieged him with letters, cables, telephone calls, all pleading for interviews. His refusals were firm. If they wanted to know about his political opinions, they could read his books or speeches. The rest of his life was his own.

He did a great deal of studying to keep up on current affairs. He also wrote several books. One of them, *Challenge of the Congo,* tells the history of the Congo from earliest times, with emphasis on the tragic sequence of events that followed the country's independence. The book is a valuable contribution to the many books produced about the Congo, because it is one of the few written from the viewpoint of

an African, and because Nkrumah personally knew Patrice
Lumumba, the Congo's former Prime Minister.

Dark Days in Ghana tells the story of the coup, the events
that led up to it, and the events that followed it. It is a
moving, sometimes harrowing story, interlined with fury and
sorrow, but written with the same confidence in the future
of his country, and of Africa, that sustained him in the past.

Class Struggle in Africa has as its thesis that the coups in
independent African countries—there were twenty-five successful ones between 1963 and 1969, including the Ghana
coup—have nearly all been the result of a union between
middle-class and wealthy Africans and foreign powers, with
the military and police merely serving as the instrument of
these forces. Nkrumah was now certain that only guerrilla
armies, composed of Africa's "workers and peasants," could
bring true democracy to a united Africa. Non-violence had
been tried. It had been found wanting. *Handbook of Revolutionary Warfare*, as the title indicates, is a manual of in-
struction for guerrilla fighters.

There is in these books a new maturity and a hardening of
Nkrumah's early convictions. His years as "Osagyefo" of the
Ghanaian people and as leader of African unity, together
with the chastening experience of his overthrow, had
changed him. He had become purely African now, a son of
ancient cultures totally foreign to the Western world.

Guinea, like Nkrumah's Ghana, was a one-party state. As
of this writing, Sékou Touré has firmly held his country together, in spite of the efforts of dissidents. Like Nkrumah,
Sékou Touré opened wide the doors to refugees and guerrilla
fighters, especially those from neighboring Portuguese
Guinea. In retaliation, there were Portuguese-sponsored raids
on Guinea territory.

On November 23, 1970, about five hundred troops were
landed in Conakry from offshore warships. They made attacks on government offices and prisons and on the Presi-

dent's residence. They killed or wounded several foreign diplomats. Civilians and Guinean troops joined together in street fighting to drive off the attackers, taking many prisoners.

President Sékou Touré, naming the Portuguese as the invaders, appealed to UN General Secretary U Thant for military aid. The Washington *Post* wrote: One is tempted to dismiss all this as a typical and fairly harmless African political charade." The government of Portugal issued a flat denial, and a Portuguese Foreign Ministry official said caustically: "The imagination of the people of the Republic of Guinea has no limits."

The UN Security Council at an emergency meeting called for immediate withdrawal of all foreign forces from Guinea and voted to send a fact-finding mission there. The mission stayed three days and interviewed a number of the prisoners. They found that no "political charade" was involved, nor "the imagination of the people of the Republic of Guinea." Their report, issued on their return, stated that the invasion "was carried out by naval and military units of the Portuguese armed forces, acting in conjunction with Guinean dissident elements from outside the Republic of Guinea."

To Kwame Nkrumah, in his Conakry villa, it must have seemed an old and familiar story.

14

GHANA WITHOUT NKRUMAH

There is so much more beyond.

—Nkrumah

Dr. Kofi A. Busia, long Nkrumah's opponent, returned from abroad after the coup to offer his services to the National Liberation Council. He wrote the preface to Afrifa's book, *The Ghana Coup,* calling it "a challenging defence of democracy." "The aim of the unconstitutional military action we took," he says in this preface, definitely involving himself with Ghana's overthrow, "is to . . . create the conditions and atmosphere in which true democracy can thrive."

There were many changes in post-Nkrumah Ghana. Most of them extended rather than diminished the undemocratic features of the last years of Nkrumah's government, an odd way to create "the conditions and atmosphere in which true democracy can thrive."

Parliament was dissolved and the self-appointed eight of the National Liberation Council ruled supreme. To have been elected to parliament was considered grounds for imprisonment. Judges and magistrates thought to be sympathetic to Nkrumah were dismissed wholesale.

Preventive detention was changed in name to "Protective Custody," with the difference that detainees did not have to be told why they were held and could make no appeal. In the first sixteen months of the new regime more political prisoners were held in protective custody than had ever been detained under preventive detention.

Right after the coup Accra newspapers were ordered to publish NLC decrees and fabricated anti-Nkrumah letters, on the threat of having their presses destroyed. Many newspaper people were fired, on the charge of being "orientated towards socialism and Nkrumaism." The Chairman of the Ghana Broadcasting Service was arrested and detained. A number of TV and radio broadcasters were ousted.

Two journalists who had been held under Preventive Detention in Nkrumah's time were made editors of the Accra *Evening News* and the *Ghanaian Times*. They promptly fell into disgrace. One of them had criticized the de-stooling of 194 chiefs so NLC appointees could replace them. The other had called for a quick return to civil government.

Foreign journalists were deported if they did not toe the line. Russian and Chinese press bureaus were closed down. An NLC decree made it a crime to utter or publish "any statement, rumor or report which is likely to cause fear or alarm or despondency to the public or to disturb the public peace or to cause dissatisfaction against the NLC."

At a press conference on May 26, 1967, General Ankrah spelled out further the NLC version of freedom of the press. He expressed indignation that Ghanaian newspapers had given headline space to the Arab-Israeli conflict. If they did not refrain "from cheap sensationalism and over-dramatizing trivial events," he warned them, then "one who pays the piper will have to call the tune." They were not to forget "that it is the government that pays their staffs."

The new Chief Justice, Eric Akufo Addo, was appointed chairman of the University of Ghana, which Nkrumah had tried to prevent from becoming a "breeding ground" of the sort of African intellectuals who worshiped Europe and despised their own people. In an address to the academic body a month after the coup, the Chief Justice said that the Uni-

versity had never had a chance to develop academic freedom, "which alone constitutes the true characteristics of a
true University." But, he added, if any of the staff had "intellectual faith in Kwame Nkrumah," they would not find
the new going "easy or congenial" and he advised them "to
be patriotic and leave the campus for the good of the campus." Thus it was made clear that the new academic freedom
stopped short of freedom to admire Nkrumah.

The NLC assumed as its primary goal the paying off of
Ghana's debts, caused, they claimed, by Nkrumah's mismanagement and personal extravagance and corruption in high
places, and amounting to sums given as 200 million pounds
at one time and 300 million at another time. The calculations
by which they arrived at these round numbers were not
revealed. Nkrumah himself was mystified by them. By a
logic all its own, the NLC reached the conclusion that the
first step in paying off the debts was to borrow more money.

NLC missions were sent abroad, "hat in hand," someone
said, to France, Britain, the United States, Germany, Italy,
Canada, Japan, Denmark. Western finance organizations,
who had refused aid to Nkrumah at the time of the disastrous drop in cocoa prices, proved friendly to the new regime.
The International Monetary Fund granted around a hundred
million dollars between May 1966 and June 1968. The International Development Association granted a fifty-year
loan of ten million dollars, interest free and with a minimal
service charge. Under the U.S. "Food for Freedom" program, five agreements were signed. The largest, dated January 3, 1968, provided for twelve million dollars' worth of
food, mostly earmarked for the needs of private Ghanaian
businessmen. Japan granted credits. Other loans were forthcoming. Some people commented that NLC Ghana was so
busy getting loans that they had no time left to spend the
money.

An austerity program was launched to balance Ghana's

budget. Education was the first to feel the hatchet. Free textbooks were eliminated. Fees for primary and secondary education were restored. School buildings under construction were left uncompleted. The plan to make Cape Coast University College a full-fledged university was abandoned.

Health facilities were cut. Many doctors resigned. Work was stopped on new hospitals. Social welfare programs were drastically reduced. The U.S. medical expert, Dr. Anna Livia Cordero of Puerto Rico, an adviser in the public health services, was forced to resign because of her criticism of NLC policies. Vital programs concerning water purification and insecticide spraying were neglected. Work was stopped on the manufacture of prefabricated houses and on other housing schemes for low-income groups. The military alone escaped the drastic cuts. In the first year of NLC rule military expenditures increased by four million pounds.

State enterprises and industries were either closed down or offered for sale to private investors. In the Accra airport, billboards which had carried anti-imperialist slogans at the time of the 1965 OAU Conference were replaced with signs welcoming foreign investors.

Some 2,500 Russian and Chinese technicians were expelled, including the Russian crew on the twenty-nine fishing trawlers Nkrumah had purchased. The trawlers themselves were sold to private concerns. Newspapers in America, Europe, South Africa, and Rhodesia hailed these developments with the headlines: "Ghana Swings to the West," and "Ghana Comes to Heel." Later on, the NLC did appeal to the Soviet Union for aid.

The military and police who had engineered the coup were the first to profit from it. As the new rulers, they could name their own salaries and promote each other to higher and higher rank. Soldiers had new equipment and guns. But the real triumph was for the wealthy African aristocracy, the Coastal Elite, who had so long opposed

Nkrumah and who had so often been thwarted by him. It was soon clear that they were the power behind the military dictatorship.

Many chiefs had welcomed Nkrumah's overthrow, thinking they would be restored to the same privileges they had had under the British. For the most part they were disappointed. Only a few of the most powerful, such as King Prempeh II of the Ashanti, had enough tribal support to make themselves felt.

The common people had been asked to tighten their belts under the Nkrumah government. Now, with the NLC austerity budget, they were expected to tighten their belts still further, with the difference that there was nothing to show for their sacrifices. Because of what Brigadier General Afrifa called "Nkrumah's inflationary policies," Ghana's currency was sharply deflated. As a result, prices of imported consumer goods rose to new heights. Some commodities vanished from the shops. A black market flourished.

In the wake of the many closed factories and halted construction projects that were a result of the NLC economy drive, tens of thousands of Ghanaians were thrown out of work. When workers went on strike, they were put down far more ruthlessly than under Nkrumah. It was now said that all strikers were "Nkrumaists."

Crime increased. A year after the coup, the *Ghanaian Times* reported that in the towns and villages of Ashanti there was a wave of terrorism "unparalleled in the history of the country," and that "in many homes there is not a wink of sleep for man or woman." (The London *Daily Telegraph* at the same time proclaimed: "Ghanaians now walk without fear.")

Stealing of food became common. School textbooks, no longer free, were stolen from warehouses. There was a rise in armed attacks and bank robberies. In March 1967, a gang of thieves raided an ammunition depot in Accra and seized a large quantity of arms and ammunition.

An attempted counter-coup against the NLC took place on April 17, 1967. It had the code name "Operation Guitar Boy." Under Lieutenant Samuel Arthur, 125 men marched from the eastern frontier more than a hundred miles to Accra. The garrison at Flagstaff House, now converted into the headquarters of Army Commander Kotoka, surrendered with no struggle. Small groups of soldiers easily occupied the strongly fortified Osu Castle (formerly Christiansborg), where General Ankrah had his headquarters, and took over the Accra airport and broadcasting station.

The NLC rallied its forces and repulsed the attackers, but not before General Kotoka was killed.

At the five-man military tribunal, Lieutenant Arthur and two others, Lieutenant Moses Yeboah and Second Lieutenant Ebenezer Osei Poku, were tried for treason. They said they had attempted their coup because the NLC packed senior ranks with their favorites and indulged in high living. Understandably, the lieutenants did not claim to be Nkrumaists. Lieutenants Arthur and Yeboah were sentenced to death and Osei Poku to thirty years' imprisonment. The executions were made a public spectacle. Some twenty thousand Ghanaians were transported to the firing grounds of the Ghana Army several miles outside Accra to witness the event.

An American seaman visited Ghana in 1968. During Nkrumah's rule, it had been his favorite port-of-call. Now he found everything different. Quaint bush-top palm-wine houses, where people could drink refreshing palm wine for two shillings, had disappeared, replaced by bars selling imported hard liquor at high prices. The Starlight Room over the Ambassador Hotel, where traditional dances were once performed, had been made into a gambling casino. A motel which had formerly rented three rooms and a bath for twelve pounds a month now charged sixty-one pounds; all the regular tenants had had to leave.

Everywhere there were armed police and soldiers. Beggars were back on the streets as in the days of colonial rule. The term "black" was in general disrepute. Nkrumah's Black Star Shipping Line was now the State Shipping Line. Billboards advertised a bleach with the slogan, "Be Beautiful by Being Light Skinned." Straight-haired wigs were fashionable.

Newspapers, television, and radio were still running a twenty-four-hour-a-day campaign against Nkrumah. A white economist broadcast that Ghana must get people back on the farms. The "industrial nonsense" Nkrumah had preached must be put out of their heads. Rubber plantations were now being run by America's Firestone Company.

The United Nations correspondent for Africa, Charles Howard, called Ghana's transformation "a holocaust." T. Peter Omari, in a book highly critical of Nkrumah's policies, conceded that Ghana, with all her rich natural resources, was "rapidly being overtaken by many of her neighbors who were considered a few years ago to be less industrious and less favored."

Rumors of corruption began to spread early. In October 1967, the *Ghanaian Times*, in an article that somehow escaped censorship, wrote that bribery and corruption "in both high and low places . . . has become unfortunately a feature of our national life." General Ankrah, Chairman of the National Liberation Council, pleaded guilty in April 1969 to accepting 30,000 Cedi (a little over $30,000) in bribes from foreign firms, in part directly, in part through an intermediary. His excuse was that he had not used the money personally but had turned it over to "various politicians." Ankrah offered his resignation, which was accepted. Brigadier General Afrifa became the new NLC chairman.

After many postponements, a constitution for the "second republic of Ghana" was drawn up. An election was called for August 29, 1969.

The two principal contenders were Dr. Kofi Busia for the Progress Party, and Komla A. Gbedemah, once Nkrumah's most trusted associate, for the National Alliance of Liberals. Like Busia, Gbedemah had returned from abroad after the coup. His party won 29 seats, mostly from the Ewe-speaking region of Trans Volta/Togo. Dr. Busia, who had support among the Ashanti and the Brong peoples, won 105 seats. He was sworn in as Prime Minister on September 3. Of all the military regimes that had taken over Africa's new nations, NLC Ghana became the first to return to civilian government.

Though Dr. Busia had supported, at least passively, the violence that constantly threatened Nkrumah and his government, he had acquired a reputation abroad as a man of peace. It was said of him that he belonged more to the leisurely nineteenth century than to the turbulent twentieth.

No one denied that he faced serious problems. In spite of the drastic economy drive, Ghana's indebtedness had increased, by a New York *Times* estimate, to a billion dollars at the end of 1969. Production of cocoa had steadily declined, in large part because of neglect in cultivation and spraying. Farmers had taken to smuggling their cocoa beans to the neighboring Ivory Coast and Togo, where they could get more money, causing an estimated loss in Ghana's foreign exchange of up to $12 million in a single year. In a population approaching nine million, some 600,000 Ghanaians were unemployed.

In mid-November, Busia's government met the crisis by issuing an edict that all aliens without a residence permit would be expelled within a week. When police declared the edict could not be enforced, the time was extended to two weeks.

The country had about two million non-Ghanaians. The freedom fighters whom Nkrumah had welcomed had long since been expelled or forced to flee. Some of the Africans who had come to work in Nkrumah's factories and building projects had stayed on. But by far the largest number of non-Ghanaians had been there for decades. They included Nigerian traders and Lebanese and Syrian merchants.

The police began making hundreds of arrests. In Kumasi and Accra, market stalls of non-Ghanaians were wrecked by citizens who believed that their misfortunes were due to foreign workers. A great exodus began, during which sick and old people died and babies were born. Near Accra airport, a huge crowd of refugees camped, waiting for transport, but authorities forced them to leave on the grounds that they were a health risk.

Some 40,000 more refugees poured over the borders into Togo, at which point the Togolese Government announced that their economy could stand no more, that only Togolese nationals would be admitted. The decision halted the progress of a line of trucks nearly two miles long approaching the frontier. The thirty or so refugees in each truck settled down to wait with the patience of the dispossessed, in the hope that the Togo authorities would relent. Friends of Prime Minister Busia claimed that he was not responsible but was the victim of circumstances. No matter how it happened, this tableau of homeless, helpless refugees was not a favorable omen for Ghana's second republic.

The government of Kofi Busia lasted only until January 12, 1972, two years and four months, when he was overthrown by Ghana's second successful military coup. Lieutenant Colonel I. K. Acheampong, leader of the revolt, accused Busia of hypocrisy, government mismanagement, corruption, malpractice, and, most ironic of all, of undermining the army's morale by taking away privileges it had enjoyed under Kwame Nkrumah.

Dr. Busia was in Britain for medical treatment at the time of the coup and did not return. The next day Acheampong arrested three other government partisans, accusing them of plotting to reinstate Busia. One was Brigadier General Afrifa, who had engineered the coup against Nkrumah. He was charged with making secret plans to fill lumber trucks with troops in Kumasi and bring them to the capital. The commander of the Kumasi army brigade and a civilian administrator in the Kumasi area were accused of being co-conspirators.

There were numerous other arrests. Some members of the Busia government were simply put under house arrest. Three soldiers were assigned to guard the villa of President Edward Akufo-Addo (whose title was as purely ceremonial as that of the King of England) "for his own protection," according to a press release.

Ghanaians accepted the new regime with resignation. They seemed drained of emotion. There is no evidence that Nkrumah's followers had any connection with Busia's overthrow, or that the coup was anything more than what it seemed—another grab for power by the military. The main difference between it and the previous coup of Afrifa, Kotoka, and Ankrah, was that Ghana's new military rulers were less actively hostile to Nkrumah. For them, he belonged to the past.

15

NKRUMAH UNFORGOTTEN

Nkrumah must come home . . . We'll go to him only
when we know his body is on Ghanaian soil.
                              —Woman merchant of Ghana

Nkrumah's prestige had been rising in the years of his exile.
The old scandals had died, like overwatered plants, of their
own exaggerations. The failures of military dictatorship had
aroused more sympathy for Nkrumah and a clearer understanding of the prodigious problems he faced in leading
the first nation south of the Sahara to be freed from colonialism. In the tense situation that enveloped Africa as one
new nation after another fell victim to plots and counter-
plots, Nkrumah's stern one-party rule was looked upon with
greater tolerance. His books met with steadily increasing
sales, in bookstores in London, Paris, and New York City, on
campuses of universities where black studies were taught,
among the young and the concerned everywhere.

Sometime during 1970, Nkrumah fell seriously ill. His
doctor diagnosed cancer. The illness was kept a strictly
guarded secret, even from many who were close to him.
Unknown to the Western world, he was flown to Eastern
Europe for treatment. For a few months he seemed to improve, but then he took a turn for the worse. Indirectly his
request was conveyed to the new Ghana Government that
he be allowed to spend his last months—or weeks—in his
home country.

Ghana's military leaders considered the request. On the one hand, a man dying of cancer could hardly be regarded as dangerous. And yet, there was always the chance that even desperately ill, he would retain his old magnetic power—that young people to whom Nkrumah was no more than a legend might succumb to "Nkrumaism," as their parents had done.

The terrible disease did not wait for the end of these deliberations. On April 27, 1972, at the age of sixty-two, Kwame Nkrumah died in a Romanian hospital. His last wish was that he be buried in Nkroful, his birthplace.

In Ghana, the government issued a statement that Nkrumah's "place in history" was assured, and ordered flags flown at half mast. But again the rulers deliberated, this time as to whether it would be safe and advisable to bring Nkrumah's body home. At last, perhaps because they feared the fury of indignant Africans, they decided to bury him. By this time Nkrumah's body had been flown back to Conakry, where President Sékou Touré had ordered three days of national mourning.

A curious diplomatic wrangle erupted. The National Redemption Council of Ghana, in a statement which spoke of Nkrumah as "the principal architect of Ghana's independence," announced on May 2 that Nkrumah's body was expected in Accra on May 15. A five-man committee of Ghanaians was sent to consult Sékou Touré on details. But Touré told them coldly that he would consider releasing Nkrumah on four conditions: that Nkrumah be rehabilitated as former Ghana President; that he be given the honors due a head of state; that all his supporters still in detention be released; that the ban on the return of the men who had stayed with him in Guinea be removed.

Negotiations were held up pending a national funeral ceremony, which began in Conakry on May 13. The ceremony coincided with the twenty-fifth anniversary of the birth of the Guinean Democratic Party. On the streets there were displays of art and dancing. "Revolutionaries don't cry over their dead," commented the chief of the Algerian delegation. "They glorify them."

The several thousand Guineans who attended the memorial service wore white—their color for mourning. Delegations came from forty different countries, inside Africa and beyond it; they represented the widest possible political spectrum from right to left.

Nkrumah's coffin, draped with the red, yellow, and green flag of Guinea, rested on one side of the auditorium of the Palace of the People. In the place of honor, next to Liberia's President, William R. Tolbert, was Madame Fathia Nkrumah, in a black mantilla and gown and wearing dark glasses. Her two sons had accompanied her from Egypt. Long before she had wanted to rejoin her husband, but he had told her to wait—to wait until he had assumed his rightful place as President of Ghana.

A nine-man delegation of Afro-Americans had come from the United States. With them was Stokely Carmichael, the American black nationalist leader, and his wife Miriam Makeba, the South African singer. They had been living in Guinea.

"Nkrumah is not a Ghanaian; he is an African," said President Sékou Touré in his ardent half-hour eulogy. "Nkrumah will never die." "Nkrumah was in the vanguard of distinguished African leaders who guided their home lands to independence," said Donald R. Norland, the American chargé d'affaires, who headed the American delegation.

After the service, Nkrumah's coffin was placed in a stadium, where at least 50,000 Guineans passed by to do homage to him. There was considerable resentment against Ghana, especially among the Guinean people, for not letting

Nkrumah spend his last days in his own country. Thus it happened that although officials were awaiting him at the Accra airport, he was buried in Conakry instead.

The arrangement proved temporary. Further negotiations took place between Guinea and Ghana. They were long and complicated but always polite. Neither country was willing to offend the other. Guinea finally yielded. His coffin was dug up and flown to Accra on July 9.

The next day, Saturday, Nkrumah's body lay in state in Accra's State House from 9 A.M. until 5:45 P.M. The entire city, even to the taxicabs, was draped in Ghana's mourning colors, red and black. Colonel Acheampong came to pay his respects early. After that the building was opened to the public. Thousands came in a line that stretched two miles long, men and women, young and old, some silent and dry-eyed, many weeping. They came for one last look at their Osagyefo, the man who had led them to independence, the man who had given them hopes of a brighter future. There could no longer be any doubt that he was not forgotten, that no one had taken his place in the hearts of the people.

On Sunday, July 11, the body was flown by helicopter some 240 miles to Nkroful, for final burial. Like Accra, this still-primitive village of mud huts with thatched roofs was decked in red and black. From all over the countryside, along narrow, winding roads, through coconut, banana, palm-nut, and rubber-tree groves, an estimated 20,000 persons came to pay their last respects.

In the combination Christian-African ceremony, chiefs and elders in native dress poured wine on the ground in a libation. Drummers beat out funeral marches. An old woman sang dirges. A Catholic bishop delivered a rather pompous eulogy, praising Nkrumah for giving "the African a personality to be proud of" and investing him "with an image of dignity and respect," but at the same time attacking him for "neglect of domestic problems" which, the bishop stated, had led to the "military take-over in 1966."

It is doubtful if anyone except foreign newspapermen sent to cover the occasion listened very closely. Attention was focused on Nkrumah's mother, aged and blind, who gently put her hand on the coffin of her son, as she had expressed a wish to do.

Soldiers in dress uniform fired their automatic rifles in a final salute. They, too, were weeping.

BIBLIOGRAPHY

Afrifa, A. A. THE GHANA COUP, FEBRUARY 24, 1966. London: Frank Cass & Company, Ltd. 1967.

Alexander, Major-General H. T. AFRICAN TIGHTROPE, My Two Years as Nkrumah's Chief of Staff. New York: Frederick A. Praeger. 1965.

Apter, David E. GHANA IN TRANSITION. New York: Atheneum. 1968.

Bing, Geoffrey. REAP THE WHIRLWIND. London: MacGibbon & Kee. 1968.

Braithwaite, E. R. A KIND OF HOMECOMING. New York: Prentice-Hall, Inc. 1962.

Bretton, Henry. THE RISE AND FALL OF KWAME NKRUMAH. New York: Frederick A. Praeger. 1966.

Campbell, Alexander. THE HEART OF AFRICA. New York: Alfred A. Knopf. 1954.

Cartey, Wilfred, and Martin Kilson. THE AFRICA READER: COLONIAL AFRICA. New York: Vintage Books (Random House). 1970.

———. THE AFRICA READER: INDEPENDENT AFRICA. New York: Vintage Books (Random House). 1970.

Davidson, Basil. AFRICA IN HISTORY. New York: The Macmillan Company. 1969.

Davidson, Basil, with F. K. Buah and the advice of J. F. Ade Ajayi. A HISTORY OF WEST AFRICA TO THE NINETEENTH CENTURY. Garden City, New York: Doubleday & Company, Inc., Anchor Books. 1966.

Fage, J. D. GHANA—A HISTORICAL INTERPRETATION. Madison, Wisconsin: The University of Wisconsin Press. 1966.

Flint, John E. NIGERIA AND GHANA. Englewood Cliffs, New Jersey: Prentice-Hall, Inc. 1966.

Legum, Colin. PAN-AFRICANISM. New York: Frederick A. Praeger. 1965.

Moore, Clark D., and Ann Dunbar, editors. AFRICA YESTERDAY AND TODAY. New York: Bantam Pathfinder Editions. 1968.

Nkrumah, Kwame. AFRICA MUST UNITE. New York: International Publishers. 1970.

———. CHALLENGE OF THE CONGO. New York: International Publishers. 1967.

———. CLASS STRUGGLE IN AFRICA. New York: International Publishers. 1970.

———. DARK DAYS IN GHANA. New York: International Publishers. 1968.

———. GHANA—THE AUTOBIOGRAPHY OF KWAME NKRUMAH. New York: Thomas Nelson & Sons. 1957.

———. HANDBOOK OF REVOLUTIONARY WARFARE. New York: International Publishers. 1969.

———. I SPEAK OF FREEDOM, A STATEMENT OF AFRICAN IDEOLOGY. New York: Frederick A. Praeger. 1961.

———. NEO-COLONIALISM, THE LAST STAGE OF IMPERIALISM. New York: International Publishers. 1966.

Nsarkoh, J. K. LOCAL GOVERNMENT IN GHANA. Accra, Ghana: Ghana University Press. 1964.

Oliver, Roland, and Anthony Atmore. AFRICA SINCE 1800. Cambridge, England: Cambridge University Press. 1969.

Omari, T. Peter. KWAME NKRUMAH, THE ANATOMY OF AN AFRICAN DICTATORSHIP. New York: Africana Publishing Corporation. 1970.

Phillips, John. KWAME NKRUMAH AND THE FUTURE OF AFRICA. New York: Frederick A. Praeger. 1960.

Robinson, Ronald, and John Gallagher. AFRICA AND THE VICTORIANS. New York: St. Martins Press. 1961.

Theobald, Robert, editor. THE NEW NATIONS OF WEST AFRICA. New York: The H. W. Wilson Company. 1960.

Timothy, Bankole. KWAME NKRUMAH. Evanston, Illinois: Northwestern University Press. 1963.

Touré, Ahmed Sékou. L'AFRIQUE ET LA RÉVOLUTION. Paris: Présence Africaine.

Wallbank, T. Walter. CONTEMPORARY AFRICA: CONTINENT IN TRANSITION. New York: D. Van Nostrand Company, Inc. 1964.

Ward, W. E. F. A HISTORY OF GHANA. London: George Allen and Unwin, Ltd. 1958.

Wiedner, Donald L. A HISTORY OF AFRICA SOUTH OF THE SAHARA. New York: Vintage Books (Random House). 1962.

Wolfson, Freda. PAGEANT OF GHANA. London: Oxford University Press. 1958.

Wright, Richard. BLACK POWER. New York: Harper & Brothers. 1954.

Bibliography

INDEX

Aborigines Rights Protection Society, 11–12, 23

Abraham, Kojo, 142

Abraham Commission, 140

Abrahams, Peter, 36, 40, 41

Accra, 5, 18, 19, 51, 55, 56, 60–61, 66, 71, 79, 86, 96, 103, 105; African Community Center, 86; All African Peoples' Conference, 123–25; Ambassador Hotel, 86; bombings (1962), 109–10; central, 104–5; Co-op Building, 105; described, 18, 104–5; Flagstaff House, 111–12, 113–14, 137–39, 142–43, 158; Independence Day Ceremonies in, 91–93; military coup and overthrow of Nkrumah in, 134–45, 154; Nkrumah's death and funeral ceremonies and, 164, 166; OAU meeting (1965) in, 131–32, riots (1948) in, 49–52; Trade Union Building, 105

Accra *Evening News*, 53, 59, 61, 62, 154

Acheampong, I. K., 161–62, 166

Achimota College, 19, 20–22, 27

Act of Independence, 82–83, 88–90

Adamafio, Tawia, 106–7, 108, 109–10

Addis Ababa, Ethiopia, 126, 130, 148

Adjei, Ako, 27, 31, 33, 42, 50, 54, 56, 106–7, 109–10, 126

Aduku Addai (chieftain), 14

Africa (*see also* West Africa; specific aspects, countries, events, individuals): First World War era,

13–24; history, 1–12; Nkrumah and anti-colonial (independence) movement in, 31–44 *passim*, 45–55, 56ff. (*see also* specific aspects, countries, individuals); Nkrumah's concern with Pan-Africanism and unity in, 21, 29, 34ff., 121–33

African Common Market, 121

African Company of Merchants, 7

African Interpreter, The (magazine), 31

African Morning Post, 22

African Students' Association, 31

Afrifa, Akwasi, 134–38, 141, 143, 153, 157, 159, 162

Aggrey, Dr. Kwegyir, 20–21, 22, 31, 34

Aggrey Students' Society, 22

Agriculture, 75–76, 81–82, 86, 115–16. *See also* Cocoa; specific aspects, individuals, organizations, people

Akan, 2ff., 7–12, 14, 20, 82–83, 84

Aksosomba, 119

Akufo-Addo, Edward, 162

Akufo Addo, Eric, 50, 154–55

Akwamu people, 5

Alexander, H. T., 111

Algeria, 122, 126

All African Peoples' Conference, 123–25

Ama Azule (river god), 15–16

Amenyah, Lieutenant, 97–100

Ametewee, Seth, 113–14

Amo, Anton Wilhelm, 14

Amponsah, R. R., 96, 97–100

Ancestor beliefs, 3, 15–16

Angola, 123

Ankrah, General J. A., 135, 136, 137, 141, 154, 158, 159, 162

Anlo Youth Organization, 84

Anti-Inflation Committee, 48

Apaloo, Modesto, 96, 97–100

Arden-Clarke, Sir Charles, 59, 68, 69, 76, 77, 81, 87–88

Armatto, Dr. Raphael, 36

Arthur, Samuel, 158

Asafu-Adjaye, E. O., 70

Asameni, 5

Asantehene (title of king of the Ashanti), 8, 9–10, 20

Ashanti, 7–12, 20, 45, 47, 51, 81, 83–85, 104, 105–6; and cocoa, 75, 82, 84–86, 94; NLC and, 157, 160; NLM and, 84–86, 94; Youth Association, 53

Ashanti Goldfields, 141

Atta, Sir Nana Ofori I, 50

Atta, William Ofori, 50, 67, 70, 80

Australia, 89

Avoidance of Discrimination Act, 96

Awhaitey, Benjamin, 97–100

Axim, 22–23

Azambuja, Don Diego d', 4

Azikiwe, Dr. Nnamdi, 22, 26, 114

Ba, Ousmane, 134

Baako, Kofi, 57, 62

Bakana (British cargo ship), 15

Bank of Ghana, 100

Barwah, Charles, 132, 135, 137

Basel Mission, 11

Belgian Congo, 124, 126–29, 139. *See also* Congo

Berbers, 1

Bing, Geoffrey, 88–89, 90, 94, 142, 144, 150

Bing, Mrs. Geoffrey, 94, 142

Black Star Shipping Line (later renamed State Shipping Line), 100, 159

Bond, Dr. Horace Mann, 73, 74

Bond of 1844, 8–9

Bonne, Nii, 48

Botsio, Kojo, 43, 54, 57, 61, 64, 70, 73, 77, 108

Braimah, Kabachewura J. A., 70, 87

Braithwaite, E. R., 104–5, 106

Britain, the British. *See* Great Britain

Brong people, 48, 160

Builders Brigade, 101

Bunche, Ralph, 75

Burns, Sir Alan (and Burns Constitution), 46, 52

Burton, Sir Richard, 22

Busia, Dr. Kofi A., 67–68, 70, 80, 83–84, 85, 94, 98, 153, 160–62

Camara, Sana, 149

Camel caravans, 1

Cameroons (Cameroun), 123, 126

Canada, 101

Cape Coast, 5, 6, 10–11, 19, 52, 62, 64

Cape Coast *Daily Mail*, 61, 62

Cape Coast University College, 117, 156

Caramansa (fifteenth-century African ruler), 4

Carmichael, Stokely, 165

Casablanca Conference (1961), 129

Casely-Hayford, A., 68–69, 70

Casely-Hayford, Joseph, 69

Ceylon, 89, 90, 129

Challenge of the Congo (Nkrumah), 150–51

Charles, Maurice, 98, 99

Chiefs (headmen), 2–3, 11–12, 19–20, 54, 66, 80–81, 82, 105–6; Joint Provincial Council of, 60–61, 80–81; and NLC, 154, 157; paramount, 3

China, 133, 143, 149, 154, 155

Chou En-lai, 133

Christianity, 3, 17, 31–32, 38. *See also* Missionaries

Christiansborg Castle (later renamed

Osu Castle), 5, 18, 49, 87–88, 93. *See also* Osu Castle (formerly Christiansborg Castle)

C.I.A.: The Inside Story, (Tully), 136

Circle, The, 41–42, 50

Class Struggle in Africa (Nkrumah), 151

Coastal Elite, 20, 23, 118; beginning of, 11–12; and NLC, 156–57; and UGCC, 42–43, 54

Cocoa, 10, 75–77, 79, 81–82, 84, 87, 116, 118–19, 144, 155, 160; NLM (formerly Council for Higher Cocoa Prices), 82, 84–86, 94; swollen shoot disease, 76, 81, 118

Cocoa Purchasing Company, 82, 87

Colonial Agricultural Loans Board, 81–82

Colonialism, Nkrumah and independence movement and, 31–44 *passim,* 45–55, 56ff., 131ff. *See also* specific aspects, countries, individuals, organizations

Colony, the. *See* Gold Coast Colony

Committee on Youth Organization, 53

Commonwealth, British, 91–102, 122–23

Communism, 40, 49, 50, 52, 53, 74–75, 115

Company of Royal Adventurers of England, 62

Conakry, 146–52; Declaration, 124–25; described, 146–47; Nkrumah's funeral ceremonies in, 164–66; Nkrumah's overthrow and exile in, 146–52

Conference of Independent African States (Leopoldville, 1960), 128

Congo, 124, 126–29, 130, 136, 150–51

Convention People's Party (CPP), 54–55, 56–65, 66–78, 79ff., 101, 105, 106–7, 110, 113, 115; election (1951), 66–78; election

(1954), 83–84; election (1956), 86; "freedom" slogan and sign of, 58, 78; organization of, 58; and overthrow of Nkrumah, 134, 138, 142, 144; party song of, 64

Cordero, Dr. Anna Livia, 156

Corruption (bribery, profiteering), 87, 106–11, 140, 159

Council for Higher Cocoa Prices (later renamed NLM), 82, 84–86, 94

Coussey (Justice Henly) Committee, 53–54, 59, 66; Constitution, 54, 59, 66, 70; Report, 59, 66

Cowper, William, *quoted,* 146

Crabbe, Coffie, 109–10

Creasey, Sir Gerald, 49, 50

Dagarti, Salifu, 114

Dagomba people, 7

Daily Telegraph, 95

Daily Worker, 40

Danes, the, 5

Danquah, Dr. Joseph B., 43, 46, 48, 50, 54, 56–57, 61, 67, 70, 107; death of, 114; and defeat for presidency in election of 1960, 102; and naming of Ghana, 82; and opposition to Volta River plan, 80; and United Party opposition, 94, 99, 102, 109

Dark Days in Ghana (Nkrumah), 151

Darku, Sir Tsibu, 61, 98, 99

Dawn Broadcast, Nkrumah's (1961), 106ff.

De Gaulle, Charles, 122–23, 125

Deku, A. K., 141

Denkyira people, 7

Deportation Act, 94–96

Diefenbaker, John George, 101

Du Bois, Dr. William E. B., 32, 35, 36

Duncan, Patrick, 124

Dutch, the, 5, 6, 7, 9

Dzewu, Dzenkle, 57

Education (schools), 10–11, 17, 18–22, 73, 87, 117–18, 144, 154–55, 156
Edusei, Krobo, 51, 57, 84, 89, 96, 108, 144
Egypt, 122, 129
Eisenhower, Dwight D., 101
Elections: (1951), 66ff.; (1954), 83–84; (1956), 85–86; (1960), 102–3; (1965), 115; (1969), 160
Elizabeth II, Queen, 91, 92
Elmina (fortress), 5, 7, 22
England (*see also* Great Britain): Nkrumah in 25–26, 33–43
Ethiopia, 16, 26, 31, 122, 126, 130
Europe(ans), 3–12, 16, 38. *See also* specific aspects, countries, events, individuals
Ewe people, 7, 94, 160
Ex-Servicemen's Union, 49

Fanti, 7, 8, 9, 11, 14, 22; Confederation, 9, 69
Fifth Pan-African Congress, 35–37
Firestone Company, 159
First Conference of Independent States (1958), 122ff.
First World War, 16–17
Fisher, George, 17
Flying Training School, 100
Foot, Dingle, 51
France (the French), 10, 15, 16, 17, 37, 39, 122–23, 125, 129, 132
Freeman, R. A., *quoted*, 45
French Community, 122–23, 129
Fry, Maxwell, 86

Gambia, 39
Gandhi, Mahatma, 37, 59, 125
Ga people, 7, 11, 50, 56, 71, 91, 96, 106–7, 109
Garvey, Marcus, 29–30
Ga Shifimo Kpee, 96, 109
Gaulle, Charles de. *See* De Gaulle, Charles

Gbedemah, Komla A., 54, 57, 62, 63, 66, 70, 77, 108, 160
Germany, 16. *See also* West Germany
Ghana (*see also* Ghana, Kingdom of; Gold Coast Colony; Nkrumah, Kwame; specific aspects, events, individuals, places); in British Commonwealth, 91–102, 122–23; coup d'état and overthrow of Nkrumah, 133, 134–45, 146–52, 153ff.; elections (*see* Elections); flag of, 92; Independence Day ceremonies, 91–92; industrialization and modernization under Nkrumah, 71ff., 79–90, 91ff., 100–3, 104–6, 115–20, 131–32; naming of, 82–83; and Nkrumah and African unity, 121–33; Nkrumah and independence for, 41–44, 45–55, 56–65, 66ff., 79ff., 91ff., Nkrumah as President of, 102–3, 104–20, 121ff.; Nkrumah as Prime Minister, 77–78, 79ff.; one-party state under rule of Nkrumah, 112–20, 121ff.; under NLC rule, 147–52, 153–62, 163ff.
Ghana, Kingdom of, 1–12, 82–83
Ghana Academy of Science, 107
Ghana Airways, 100
Ghana Congress Party, 83–84
Ghana Coup (Afrifa), 153
Ghana-Guinea Union, 124–25, 129
Ghana National College, 52
Ghana People's Representatives, 59
Ghana Youth Association, 53, 54
Ghanian Times, 154, 157, 159
Ghartey IV, King (of Winneba), 9
Gold (gold mining), 1, 3–6, 7, 10, 72, 84, 95, 116, 141
Gold Coast Colony, 9–12, 81 (*see also* Ghana; Ghana, Kingdom of); British and (*see* Great Britain); First World War era and, 13–24; Nkrumah and independence for, 37–44, 45–55, 56–65, 66–90 *pas-*

sim, 91–93; Nkrumah as Prime Minister of, 77–78, 79ff.; Nkrumah's birth, background, and education in, 13–24
Golden Stool, the, 7–8, 10
Government Training College, Nkrumah at, 18–19
Grant, George A. ("Pa Grant"), 42
Great Britain, 5, 6–12, 16, 18, 19, 36, 39, 91ff., 122, 142 (*see also* Commonwealth British; Gold Coast Colony; specific aspects, events, individuals, issues); and Indirect Rule, 19–20, 23, 94; Nkrumah and Ghana independence movement and, 41–44, 45–55, 56–65, 66–78, 79ff., 91ff.
Guggisborg, Sir Gordon, 19, 20, 25, 79
Guinea, 122–23, 124, 126, 129, 148–52, 164–66; Nkrumah's exile in, 146–52

Haile Selassie, 26, 31
Hamilton, John, 387
Hammarskjöld, Dag, 128
Handbook of Revolutionary Warfare (Nkrumah), 151
Hanoi, Nkrumah in, 132–33
Harlley, John W. K., 114, 132, 135–36, 137, 141
Hasan, Brigadier, 137
Hausa people, 95, 96
Health (medical) programs, Nkrumah and, 116–17, 156
Ho Chi Minh, 132
Hodgson, Sir Frederic, 10
Holden, Roberto, 123
Houphoet-Boigny, Félix, 39
Housing, 86, 104–5, 131–32
Howard, Charles, 159
Howard University, 32
Hutton Mills, T., 70

Impellitteri, Vincent, 75

Independence (independence movement), 37–44, 45–55, 56–65, 66–90 *passim;* ceremonies in Accra to celebrate, 91–93; granting of, 91–93
Independence Day, 91–93
India, 37, 60, 96, 97, 98, 101, 102, 125
Indirect Rule, 19–20, 23, 94
Industrialization (and modernization), 91, 100–3, 104–6, 114–20, 131–32
Institute of African Languages and Culture, 31
International Development Association, 155
International Monetary Fund, 155
Israel, 100, 142
Ivory Coast, 15, 39, 160

James Fort Prison, Nkrumah in, 62, 63–64, 69
Janssens, Émile, 127
Johnson, George, 26–27, 29, 31–32
Johnson, Wallace, 36, 40
Joint Provincial Council of Chiefs, 60–61, 66
Jones, Arthur Creech, 49

Kasai Province, 127, 128
Kasavubu, Joseph, 127
Katanga Province, 127
Keita, Modibo, 129
Kenya, 98, 123
Kenyatta, Jomo, 36, 41–42
Koi, Dr. Ansah, 70
Korsah, Sir Arku, 110–11
Kotoka, E. K., 134–38, 141, 143, 158
Kulungugu plot, 109–11
Kumasi, 8, 9, 10, 19, 20, 47, 50–51, 82, 95, 105–6, 161–62; College of Technology, 87; Cultural Center, 105–6; described, 105–6

Lamptey, Obetsebi, 50, 56–57, 94, 109–10
Lands Bill, 11–12, 23
Laski, Harold, 35, 36
League of Nations, 16
Legislative Assembly, 66, 71, 77–78, 79–80, 85, 87, 88, 92 (*see also* Legislative Council; National Assembly; Parliament); Nkrumah's "Motion of Destiny" speech to, 82–83
Legislative Council, 19, 59, 61, 66ff. *See also* Legislative Assembly
Legon, University College of Ghana at, 87
Lennox-Boyd, A. T., 85
Leopoldville, 128–29
Liberia, 16, 43–44, 122, 125, 129, 165
Lie, Trygve, 75
Lincoln Theological Seminary, 30–32
Lincoln University (Pa.), 23–24, 26–30, 73–74
Liverpool, Nkrumah in, 25–26
London, Nkrumah in, 26, 33, 35–43
London *Daily Telegraph*, 143–44, 157
London School of Economics, 35
London *Times*, 143
Lumumba, Patrice, 124, 126–29, 151

MacDonald, Ramsay, 36
Maclean, Captain George, 8
Madagascar, 126
Madjitey, Eric, 114
Makeba, Miriam, 165
Malaria, 5, 11, 116
Mali, 129, 134
Manchester, England, Fifth Pan-African Congress in, 35–37
Mboya, Tom, 123
Missionaries, 10–11, 17, 38
Mobutu, Joseph, 128, 129, 136
Monkrong, 130

Monrovia, Liberia, 43–44
Morocco, 122, 129
Moslem Association Party, 84
Moslems, 2, 84, 122, 146
"Motion of Destiny" speech, Nkrumah's (July 10, 1953), 82–83
Moumie, Dr. Félix, 123
Mouvement National Congolese (National Congolese Movement), 124
Mussolini, Benito, 26

Nasser, Gamal A., 94, 138
National Alliance of Liberals, 160
National Assembly, 110, 112, 113. *See also* Legislative Assembly
National Liberation Council (NLC), 141–45; Ghana under rule of, 147–52, 153–62, 163–67; and overthrow of Nkrumah, 141–45
National Liberation Movement (NLM, formerly Council for Higher Cocoa Prices), 84–86, 94
National Redemption Council, 164
Nehru, Pandit, 101, 102
Neo-Colonialism, Last Stage of Imperialism (Nkrumah), 131
New African, The (monthly review), 39
New Delhi, University of, 101
New York, Nkrumah in, 26, 27, 74, 75
New York *Times*, 140
Nigeria, 39, 126
Nikoe, Ashie, 57
Nixon, Richard M., 91
Nkroful, 13ff., 18, 139, 166–67
Nkrumah, Gorke Gamal (son), 94
Nkrumah, Kwame: achievements under, 71ff., 79–90, 91ff., 100–3, 104–6, 115–20, 131–32 (*see also* specific aspects, kinds); arrest and imprisonment of, 50–52, 62–65, 66–70ff.; birth, childhood, and education of, 13–24, 34ff.; called Osagyefu, the Redeemer, 59,

107, 151, 166; conspiracies and plots against, 94–100, 101, 107ff., 113–14, 132ff.; coup d'état and overthrow of, 133, 134–45, 146–52ff.; death and burial of, 163–67; described, personality, habits, 21, 28, 29, 47–48, 71–72, 93, 111–12; and elections (*see* Elections); exile of, 146–52ff., 163–67; and independence movement (*see* Independence [Independence movement]); Leader of Government Business, 69–78; myths about, 58–59, 63, 72, 142–45; one-party state in Ghana and rule of, 112–20, 121ff.; parents (mother), 14–15, 16, 17, 18, 45, 93, 138–39, 167; political thinking of, 29–33, 34–44, 45–55, 56ff., 121–33 (*see also* specific aspects, events, issues); popularity with people, 47–48, 58, 68, 72; and Positive Action, 59–65, 66–78, 79, 125; as President, 102–3, 104–20, 121ff.; as Prime Minister, 77–78, 79ff., 91ff.; and public speaking, 22, 32, 40, 45–55, 82–84, 106–7; and religion, 17, 30, 31–32; and Tactical Action, 79–90; writings of, 38–39, 40, 53, 131, 150–51, 163

Nkrumah, Madame Kwame (*née* Fathia Helen Ritzk), 93, 94, 138, 165

Nkrumah, Samia Yabah (daughter), 94

Nkrumah, Seku Ritzk (daughter), 94

Nkrumaism, 117–20, 154, 164

Norland, Donald R., 165

North Africa, 1

Northern People's Party, 83–84, 94

Northern Territories, 8, 10, 18, 47, 51, 81, 83–84, 92, 106, 136–37

Nunoo, J. E., 141

Nyerere, Julius, 123

Nzima, 14, 15–16, 22–23, 56

Nzima Literature Society, 22–23

O'Brien, Conor Cruise, 118

Ocran, A. K., 1

Omari, T. Peter, 159

"Operation Guitar Boy," 158

Organization of African Unity (OAU), 130–33, 148, 156

Osu Castle (formerly Christiansborg Castle), 111, 158. *See also* Christiansborg Castle (later renamed Osu Castle)

Otu, Major General, 135

Padmore, George, 34, 35, 40

Pan-Africa (magazine), 40

Pan-Africanism, 30, 35–37, 40, 121–33

Parliament, 94, 97–98. *See also* Legislative Assembly

Pennsylvania, University of, 31, 32

Philadelphia, Pa., Nkrumah in, 32, 34

Philosophy and Opinions of Marcus Garvey, 29

Plange, Kwesi, 57, 64, 66

Poku, Ebenezer Osei, 158

Portugal (the Portuguese), 3–5, 123, 147, 151–52

Portuguese Guinea, 147, 151–52

Positive Action, 37, 59–65, 66–78, 79, 125

Powell, Erica, 79

Prempeh I, King, 9–10, 20

Prempeh II, King, 20, 84, 157

Presidential Election Act (May 1965), 115

President's Guard, 111, 137, 138

Preventive Detention Act, 96, 97–100, 109, 113, 114, 139–40, 153–54

Prisons Act, 113

Progress Party, 160

Quaison-Sackey, Alex, 132

Quashie, Tetteh, 75

Quist, Sir Emmanuel, 71, 77, 84

Rhodesia, 130
Roads (road-building), 115
Robeson, Paul, 32
Romans, ancient, 1
Roosevelt, Franklin D., 27, 34
Royal Adventurers of England Trading to Africa, 6–7
Royal African Company, 7
Russia. *See* Soviet Union

Sahara Desert, 1, 21
Saloway, R. H., 60
Saltpond, 46–47, 50, 52
Sanniquellie Declaration, 125
Savundra, Emil, 95–96
Scott, Michael, 124, 125
Sears, Sir Edward, 141
Second Conference of Independent African States, 125–26
Second Five Year Development Plan, 101–2, 106, 115–20
Second World War, 30, 34, 45
Security Service Act (1963), 113
Sekondi *Morning Telegram,* 61
Sekondi-Takoradi railway strike (1951), 107–8
Senegal, 39
Senghor, Léopold, 39
Sharp, Gilbert Granville, 98, 99
Shawnee (ship), Nkrumah employed aboard, 28
Sierra Leone, 39, 147
Slavery (slave trade), 5–8, 24
Sleeping sickness (trypanosomiasis), 116
Socialism, 117. *See also* Communism
Somalia, 126
South Africa, 10, 91, 124, 130
Soviet Union, 75, 108, 115, 123, 143, 144, 154, 155
Spaniards, the, 5
Strikes, 107–11, 157
Sudan (the Sudanese), 1, 2, 122, 126
Sule, Yussuf Maitma, 126
Swedes, the, 5, 6
Swiss Basel Mission, 11

Tactical Action, 79–90
Takordi, 80; Harbor, 25, 86, 100, 107
Tamale, Northern Territories, 47, 51, 136–37
Tano River, 15
Tanzania, 123
Tarkwa, 45, 46
Tema, 80, 119; Harbor, 120
Thompson, Thomas, 10–11
Togo, 160, 161. *See also* Togoland; Trans Volta/Togo territory
Togoland, 16–17, 84, 88, 94. *See also* Togo
Togoland Party, 84
Tolbert, William R., 165
Torrane, Colonel, 8
Touré, Madame Andrée Sékou, 149
Touré, Sékou, 123, 124, 129, 151–52; and death of Nkrumah, 164, 165; and Nkrumah's exile, 147, 148, 149
Toward Colonial Freedom (Nkrumah), 38–39
Trade Union Council, 107–8
Trans Volta/Togo territory, 16–17, 88, 160, 161
Tshombe, Moise, 127, 128
Tuaregs, the, 21
Tubman, William, 43, 125
Tully, Andrew, 136
Tunisia, 122, 128, 129
Tuskegee Institute, 52

Uganda, 140
Union of West African Socialist Republics, 52
Union of West African States, 123
United Ghana Farmers' Council, 107
United Gold Coast Convention (UGCC), 42–43, 44–55, 56ff., 80, 94, 98, 107, 109–10; Convention Party and, 54–55, 56–58, 67; and election of 1951, 67, 71; and election of 1954, 83–84; organization

and program of, 46–47

United Nations, 34, 75, 88, 126, 127–28, 129; and Congo, 127–28, 129; Declaration of Human Rights, 122; and Guinea, 152; OAU and, 130

United Party, 94–101, 102–3, 110–11

United States, 91, 101, 123, 132, 140, 142, 149, 150, 155, 165; Central Intelligence Agency, 136; Nkrumah at school in, 25–33; Nkrumah's visit to (1951), 74–75

Universal Negro Improvement Association, 29

University of Ghana, 117, 118, 154–55

U Thant, 152

Vietnam, 132–33

Volta River, S.S., 100

Volta River Dam (hydroelectric project), 79–80, 101, 119–20

Washington, Booker T., 52

Watson, Aiken (Watson Commission), 51–52, 53–54

Welbeck, N. A., 57

Wells, H. G., 36

West Africa: Gold Coast before Nkrumah and, 1–12; Nkrumah and independence movement, 30, 35ff. (*see also* Independence [independence movement]); Nkrumah and unity of states in, 35ff., 121–33 (*see also* Pan-Africanism)

West African Conference, 39, 44

West African National Secretariat, 37–39, 121

West African Students' Union, 34, 39–40

West Germany, 142

Williams, H. Sylvester, 35

Winneba, 6, 9, 117

Wood, Dr. Samuel R., 23

Workers Brigade, 101, 116

Wright, Richard, 17, 32

Yajubu, B. A., 141

Yaméogo, Maurice, 109

Yeboah, Moses, 158

Young Pioneers, 101

Youth Study Group, 53

Zaïre, 129

Zanerigu, Colonel, 137

"Zeriken Zongo," 95

Zwichanko, Constantine, 75

Robin McKown was born in Denver, Colorado, and spent her childhood vacations in a ghost mining town (population 37) high in the Rocky Mountains. She is a graduate of the University of Colorado, attended Northwestern University School of Drama for a year, and spent another year at the University of Illinois. At Colorado, the Little Theatre produced her first literary effort—a one-act poetic drama. After her marriage she moved to New York, and had a miscellaneous assortment of jobs, including seven years with Book-of-the-Month Club writing book reviews and radio scripts.

Writing books for young people has been a full-time occupation for the last dozen years and has involved considerable travel. Out of an extended stay in the northern mining region of France came *Janine* (which won the 1961 Child Study Association award) and a boy's story, *Patriot of the Underground*. She went to Peru to get material for *The Story of the Incas*, and to Madagascar for background for three books on that little-known island: *Rakoto and the Drongo Bird, The Boy Who Woke Up in Madagascar*, and *Girl of Madagascar*. Part of research for *Lumumba* was done in Zaïre, the former Belgian Congo. Research for *Nkrumah* involved a trip to Ghana. At present Mrs. McKown lives on a 97-acre farm, mostly wooded hills, in western New York State.